CONSIDER YOURSELF BLESSED
How to Walk in the Blessings of God Every Day

ARAMA CHRISTIANA

Copyright © 2020 by Arama Christiana

This book is protected by the copyright laws of the United States of America. This book or any part of this book and/or the cover may not be copied or reprinted for commercial gain or profit, stored in a retrieval system, or transmitted in any form or means – mechanical, electronically, photocopy, recording, etc. The use of short quotations or copying of a page for personal or study groups is permitted and encouraged. Other permissions can be granted on individual request by the author.

"Unless otherwise stated, all Scripture quotations are taken from the New American Standard Bible®, (NASB)

Copyright © 1960, 1962, 1963, 1968, 1971, 1972, 1973, 1975, 1977, 1995 by The Lockman Foundation Used by permission." (www.Lockman.org)

"Scripture quotations marked (AMP) are taken from the Amplified® Bible, Copyright © 1954, 1958, 1962, 1964, 1965, 1987 by The Lockman Foundation Used by permission." (www.Lockman.org).

ISBN: 9798642361146

All rights reserved.

In Loving Memory of
Adela Jones
Florence Ademu-John
Miriam Cole

The Blessings of God

25 The Lord bless you, and keep you [protect you, sustain you, and guard you]; 25 The Lord make His face shine upon you [with favor], And be gracious to you [surrounding you with lovingkindness]; 26 The Lord lift up His countenance (face) upon you [with divine approval], And give you peace [a tranquil heart and life].
Numbers 6:24-26 (AMP)

6 but showing graciousness and steadfast lovingkindness to thousands [of generations] of those who love Me and keep My commandments.
Exodus 20:6 (AMP)

Topics in this Book

Copyright.. ii
Dedication..iii
The Blessings of God iv
Is There A Problem?................................ 1
My Story And Why I Wrote This Book............... 7
What This Book Will Do For You 15
Who Are You?...................................... 21
Analyze Your Situation 29
Survey/Check Your Reality 39
Uncover Your Roots 55
Identify Blessing Blockers 59
Pull Down Strongholds............................ 83
God Has Regarded You 87
Prayer of Repentance 93
Renew Your Mind 97
Know Who You Are In Christ 101
Know the Power In His Blood 103
Annihilate Your Gideon Complex 107
Spend Time In His Presence 117
Meditate On And Speak His Word................. 121
See It How God Sees It 125
Shift Your Paradigm 133
Expect "An Expected End" 137

CHAPTER 1
Is There A Problem?

*My people are destroyed for lack of knowledge
[of My law, where I reveal My will].
Hosea 4:6 (AMP)*

Are you frustrated with the way things are in your life? Do you find it hard to grasp or believe that God really means well for you? Are God's promises absent from your life?

If you answered yes to any or all of the above questions and you are desperate to understand why and change things for the better, then stay tuned. Don't give up!

I am about to share with you simple but very important steps you can take and do every day to start living the life of abundance God promises in the Bible. What you need, is to understand, get a hold of God's expectations and plans, and simply put them into effect by applying them to your life.

God wants you blessed and living a full life. His desire is for you to walk in all that He has provided for you through

His Son's death on the cross. God wants you to experience abundant life.

For clarity, when I use the word "blessing" or "prosperity" throughout this book, I am not merely talking about financial gain and financial independence. I am referring to all aspects of your life (spiritual, physical, financial, emotional, and mental).

No matter what you're going through, the answer lies in God's instructions and His provisions, in the Bible, which assures us that nothing is impossible with God (Luke 1:37).

The basic foundation and reason for your frustration and lack may stem from a number of things, which we will touch on in order to help fix your current situation. It may, however, be from the simple fact that you do not know God, Himself, as stated in Hosea 4:6, the scripture referenced at the beginning of this chapter.

Hosea 4:6 is God's cry because His children, meaning you and I, are perishing, suffering because the very thing that would save us is knowing our Father's thoughts and desires and His will for our individual lives.

There is hope. It is in the Bible, the Word of God. You have to read and study the Bible to know what God's thoughts are toward you in order to walk in the manner God intended for each and every one of His children. If you are ignorant or clueless of your inheritance, and you do not know Who your Heavenly Father is, then how do you know what is available to you?

Is There A Problem?

As Christians, it is important that we align our thoughts, our words and actions with those of our Heavenly Father, whether our need is in the area of healing, deliverance, forgiveness, blessing or holiness. God shows us and tells us how He expects us to react in every one of these situations simply because He wants us blessed, in every possible way, and living a victorious and holy life.

Perhaps like most Christians, you have already considered yourself less than a person whom God would want to bless. You feel undeserving or incapable of a close relationship with God. You think that making an impact on your family, let alone the world or your surroundings/neighborhood, is for those fortunate few or high-profile evangelists and pastors. That is not the case, but rest assured, you are not alone in your thinking.

Many people exist in a mediocre relationship with God, seeking Him only when they are desperate and in the depths of despair. They stand by, waiting and hoping He answers. They get to a point in their Christian walk where they are so bogged down with the distractions and disappointments of life that it shatters the very foundation on which they stand.

If not careful, this attitude, this concept, leads to a deep, dark place, where every step becomes a fight for survival. Could that be how you feel?

I know because I have been there.

Things can get so bad for the individual who thinks they have been left out of God's promises that all they see and believe is that everyone else is moving forward, increasing by leaps and bounds while they are stuck in a rut. For this reason, most of us do not reach our full potential in Christ because of such skewed thinking. We believe that the blessings that God has provided do not apply to us, and therefore, we do not partake in His provisions laid out for His children.

There are also other reasons why you may not be operating in the full capacity as a child of God. This includes but is not limited to the categories below as the list can be an extensive one.

You may be:
- clueless of the Bible's promises and that all the blessings you will ever need have already been provided for you to claim (Hosea 4:6), or
- clueless to your entitlement as a child of God and joint heir with Jesus Christ (Romans 8:17), or
- operating from things you've heard others declare and say over you (or about you) or things that happened to you at a young age or, more recently, that have shattered your foundation (Ecclesiastes 7:21), or
- lacking the lushness/richness in which you once walked because, somewhere along the way, you lost sight of, or broke covenant with God. (Jeremiah 2:2)

Sadly enough, even as God's children and despite His instructions and provisions, we choose to believe the lies of the enemy and the lies of others rather than the truth of our Father's words.

Let me say it again. God wants you blessed and living a life of abundance and victory.

17 And if [we are His] children, [then we are His] heirs also: heirs of God and fellow heirs with Christ [sharing His spiritual blessing and inheritance], if indeed we share in His suffering so that we may also share in His glory.
Romans 8:17 (AMP)

Personal/Additional Notes:

CHAPTER 2
My Story And Why I Wrote This Book

8 For it is by grace [God's remarkable compassion and favor drawing you to Christ] that you have been saved [actually delivered from judgment and given eternal life] through faith. And this [salvation] is not of yourselves [not through your own effort], but it is the [undeserved, gracious] gift of God; 9 not as a result of [your] works [nor your attempts to keep the Law], so that no one will [be able to] boast or take credit in any way [for his salvation].
Ephesians 2:8-9 (AMP)

Growing up in Freetown, Sierra Leone, I had a beautiful relationship with my Heavenly Father. I was confident that I was highly favored, blessed and loved most dearly of God. It was as if I had been born with that knowledge engraved in the core of my heart. It was not in an obnoxious or arrogant manner. I was very young at the time and knew nothing else but that God loved me very much; and I in return, loved Him most ardently indeed. In my then innocence, I thought every person in the Universe experienced God the exact same way I experienced Him.

I owe that youthful, confident regard of myself to three women; my maternal great grandmother and both my paternal and maternal grandmothers. These three powerful women of God stirred up and nurtured my young spirit. Each, in her own way, assured me of God's unwavering and unconditional affections for me and just how much I meant to Him and to them.

Each invested in my life more than I realized back then. I will forever be grateful to them for that. They made me understand the depth of God's love toward me and that He had already considered me favorably and had blessed me beyond my wildest imaginations, and that there was nothing I lacked. They made me believe that whatever my need, He had already provided; and whatever I wanted, if I asked God, He would give it to me.

That concept, that thinking was ingrained in me from my infancy.

Not that my life was and is without hang-ups, hiccups and glitches; but from a very young age, I was at peace with God. I knew that He had my back. I would even warn people not to fight with me because God loved me so much that He fought my battles and would reprimand anyone who dared to come against me.

At that early age, I had also learned to spend time with God and would wait until late at night when everyone was asleep to sneak into the sitting room and worship and fellowship with Him.

So, if I had such a great relationship with my Heavenly Father, what happened? What do I know about being stuck in a rut and not walking in His provisions?

Well, fast forward years later. As a young adult, I started attending churches that based one's wellbeing on works. I got blinded to the truths in the scriptures and started questioning everything. I second-guessed whether or not I should pray for a need, and if I did pray, doubted whether I would receive. Moreover, I questioned whether I had earned the right to even pray for anything.

I allowed the negative vibes and experiences from other Christians to influence the foundation my grandparents had established. I started focusing on how good I had to be rather than what Jesus had already done for me on the cross.

I overlooked the fact that Ephesians 2:8-9 confirms that it was *by His grace I had been saved and that it was through faith, not by what I had done or what I would do*—that my salvation and those benefits were given to me as gifts from God. They were not by my doings, so I had no grounds for boasting.

The truth of that scripture became clouded by bad teachings. Those negative teachings and the works mentality chipped away at my confidence and ultimately caused me to doubt my position as a child of God and joint recipient of my inheritance with Christ Jesus.

Doubting my ability and eligibility to receive from God soon spilled into every area of my life. Soon that confident 18-year-old from Africa (me) became someone hoping her prayers would get answered, begging and pleading with God for things He had already handed over to me, things which, in the past, I would have known were already mine.

I stopped praying and believing in faith. My words changed, and with that, heavenly portals, once open wide and at my grasp, closed. I no longer thought I had the access or freedom to walk into my Father's throne room and receive from Him.

When I started agreeing with the negative beliefs of other Christians, things turned for the worse. I began to struggle in ways I never imagined possible. All of this was due to what I like to call "stinking thinking" of religious folk.

I became doubtful, uncertain, and confused.

I was like the daughter of a billionaire who could no longer live off of her inheritance because she doubted if it really belonged to her.

One pastor had had it with me. He reprimanded me for being too expectant of God's provisions. He let me know in no uncertain terms that it was wrong for me to think so highly of myself and that I needed to be humble; in essence, he said I was being blasphemous.

My friend, let me tell you that knowing and believing who you are in Christ Jesus, knowing that you are loved and favored by Him, is neither heresy nor arrogance. It is your inheritance. Your right. It is a confident knowing that so many Christians lack but need to acquire.

God loves me. God loves you. That is neither heresy nor blasphemy. God loves us and proved it when He sacrificed His only Son to die for you and me. It was a pure display of the extent of His affection toward us as stated in Colossians.

When He had disarmed the rulers and authorities [those supernatural forces of evil operating against us], He made a public example of them [exhibiting them as captives in His triumphal procession], having triumphed over them through the cross.
Colossians 2:15 (AMP)

God disarmed and publicly shamed and exposed the enemy, the liar, our accuser, so that we would bear no shame but stand in the love God has for us and we for Him.

We need to know who we are in God, and in His Son, Jesus, the Christ.

It is wise to study and know the Word of God intimately and meditate upon His truth in order to protect His anointing in and upon your life. Otherwise, man-made words, man-made rules and regulations, and man-made religion can destroy Godly foundations. You always need to protect God's anointing over you.

Don't get me wrong. The Christians I encountered and fellowshipped with were sweet and sincere, albeit sincerely deceived. They literally destroyed the foundation on which I stood.

No longer was I confident of my position in Christ. My way of thinking changed.

Proverbs 23:7 tells us that a man is the exact representation of his thoughts.

In earlier days, everything was possible and reachable and obtainable because I knew that I had already received all that God had for me. I had possessed a stubborn confidence of that truth.

Aligning my way of thinking with others, rather than with Gods' regard for me, set me so far back that it was an unbelievably long, hard road to recovery. With this new lack of confidence and shifted thinking, I became doubtful, uncertain, and confused. I started trying to work out my righteousness in order to justify writing a withdrawal request against my inheritance.

When you have money in the bank, you do not call and beg the banker to give it to you, do you? You walk in without hesitation, provide proof of who you are and withdraw exactly what you need. It is the same principle with God. When you know who you are in Him, you approach life with a confident regard of yourself.

When you know who you are in Christ Jesus, when you understand exactly who God says you are, and the power you possess, and all that is at your fingertips, you can confidently tell anyone who appears before you speaking lies about how you have to work and earn God's love, favor, and blessings that they have come too late to persuade you otherwise. You can say with confidence that you choose to trust God.

To be honest, I can only put so much blame on the people I fellowshipped with back then. I must own up to my part. It was my mistake. I allowed it—allowed their words, their teachings, and their beliefs to enter and corrupt my spirit and my thoughts. Perhaps it was due to my youthfulness, but I was the one who did not protect God's anointing in me nor guarded my early teachings.

Listening to the lies of others, particularly those we trust for guidance and support in our Christian walk, can become very detrimental, especially to young believers. It took years to shake off cockeyed ways of thinking, retrace my steps, and rebuild those early foundational truths. But, I did it! I recovered and so can you.

You can choose to believe in God's word and trust Him. He means well for you. You can say with confidence that as for you and your household, He, God, is the one Whom you serve (Joshua 24:15).

Trust in the Lord with all your heart
And do not lean on your own understanding.
In all your ways acknowledge Him,
And He will make your paths straight.
Proverbs 3:5-6

Personal/Additional Notes:

CHAPTER 3
What This Book Will Do For You

For I know the thoughts that I think toward you, saith the Lord, thoughts of peace, and not of evil, to give you an expected end.
Jeremiah 29:11

The purpose of this book is to provide you with mind-renewing tools and activities that will let you see yourself the way God sees you. Armed with the knowledge gained, you can rise up to be the man or woman God has already declared you to be. In addition, applying the principles outlined in the Bible to your life will empower you to walk in all Godly provisions laid out for you. God's thoughts and plans for you are all good, and He tells you so in Jeremiah 29:11. Stop and think about that for a moment.

If you have not already studied Jeremiah 29:11, memorize it and meditate on it until its truth is engraved in the very core of your being.

Jeremiah clearly states that God has good thoughts for you and clarifies further, what those good thoughts encompass, which is for you to have peace and hope and a blessed future until the end of your life—and that you can expect even the end of your days to be filled with goodness.

The King James version calls this an "expected end." The phrase "expected end" denotes an outcome or result that is not a surprise. What is your expected end? Better yet, what is God's expected end for you?

In fact, there are many scriptures in the Bible that indicate how God expects us to live to the very end of our lives. One example is in Psalm 23. Although most of us know the 23rd Psalm well and have memorized and repeated it so many times, I think the impact of the protection and the meanings and intentions of the scripture have lessened over time due to the familiarity and frequency with which it is loosely spat out.

I challenge you to take the time to slowly read through Psalm 23, chew on it, digest it and let the meaning of each sentence, sink into your heart.

Verse 6 of Psalm 23 states that most definitely goodness and mercy shall follow you. It does not end there nor do the words denote a temporary condition, but the scripture goes further and tells you when that (goodness and mercy) will occur, which is, all the days of your life. What better insurance than that? So, it is not just today or tomorrow, but an expectation that even your last days on earth will be filled with goodness and mercy.

For that reason alone, when people ask me what my sign is or they want to read me a fortune cookie or horoscope that will predict how my life or my day would go, I inform them that I already know my sign and it is in the cross of Christ Jesus. I inform them that it is already established in God's Word, in Psalm 23:6, that most definitely, His goodness and lovingkindness will follow me all the days of my life. All, in this case, meaning every day. That is my ascertained fortune. It is my expected end. It is yours as well.

We need to be careful that we are following God's Words, His path, and not what man dictates.

When you are fed the wrong information, when you remove your eyes from God's provisions and become dependent on your merits and on man's words, it becomes difficult to trust God and to believe He means well for you.

The same thing happened when Paul saw that Peter and the other disciples had come up with all these rules and regulations for their fellow Christians to follow. All it did was put a burden on believers and set them up for failure right from the word "Go!"

You are the reason I wrote this book. Wherever you are in your walk with God, I want to assist in opening your eyes to the truth of God's words, and so strengthen and help you fix the cracks, if your foundation has been shattered. I want to encourage you to see yourself in God's light and in all that God has already declared of you.

Not only do I want you to see it, I want you to know it to the depth of your core. To walk it. To talk it. To live it. To have all of God's goodness engraved and rooted deep in your heart.

It is time to step into and walk in all the fullness God has for your life. It is time to take back your stance and fulfill your calling and your destiny. There is no more time to waste wondering or thinking about it.

Can you afford to live in defeat another day, another month or years? Can you stand to see your loved ones defeated and depressed when they could walk victoriously in Christ? I don't think so.

I want you to understand exactly what is at stake by not aligning your thoughts with God's thoughts and by not coming into agreement with God's word. After reading and studying the concepts in this book, you will be able to:

- assess and evaluate who you are and where you stand,
- pressure-test any circumstance against God's word,
- know God's regard for you as His child, and
- learn simple steps to fix the gaps you discover between your thinking and God's intentions for your life.

In turn, you will also be able to:

- rightly utilize God's Word for a renewal of your mind, and
- most importantly, learn how to maintain and protect the anointing for a life full of His blessings.

Breaking through and obtaining and establishing God's provisions in your life goes far beyond your current situation. The breakthroughs you receive, will without a doubt, transfer down to your children and your children's children for generations to come, until the coming of Jesus Christ.

> *...but showing graciousness and steadfast lovingkindness to thousands [of generations] of those who love Me and keep My commandments.*
> *Exodus 20:6 (AMP)*

This book is designed to encourage you to discover Godly solutions for change. My prayer is that its content will provoke you to seek and cash in on all that God has prepared and stored up for you. I pray that it will awaken and stir up a desire within you to walk every day in God's blessings and favor.

I pray that you will act on and implement guidelines and recommendations outlined in the next few chapters so that you can experience God's blessings and untold riches in every area of your life (spiritual, mental, emotional, physical, and financial) and the lives of your loved ones for God's blessings do not bring nor result in sadness (Proverbs 10:22).

I pray that you examine the scriptures and ask God for His divine wisdom and for a heart that knows and understands God's Word and is willing to implement His principles.

Seeing how God, your Father, has already considered you is important for a life full of joy, satisfaction and contentment—a life with an expected end—a life where God's peace in you surpasses human comprehension.

The blessing of the Lord brings [true] riches, And He adds no sorrow to it [for it comes as a blessing from God].
Proverbs 10:22 (AMP)

Personal/Additional Notes:
_____
_____
_____
_____
_____
_____
_____
_____
_____
_____
_____
_____
_____
_____

CHAPTER 4
Who Are You?

See how great a love the Father has bestowed on us, that we would be called children of God; and such we are. For this reason the world does not know us,
because it did not know Him.
1 John 3:1

I never got to meet my paternal grandfather, but I heard lots of great things about him. He and my grandmother had ten children. He was a preacher, a man who was very serious about his faith and his God. He was a hard-worker who cared for his family and for others. He bought a piece of land which he cultivated and developed into an orchard farm. When he died, my grandmother was left to take over the affairs of the estate and deal and negotiate with the many merchants who came daily to purchase produce.

When a merchant and his workers or family had been given the okay by my grandmother, they would walk the grounds, picking and gathering items for which they had obtained agreement from my grandmother to purchase.

At the end of their time at the farm, they would return with their goods and set it in front of my grandmother and proceed to count out dozens of whatever they had picked; mangoes, oranges, guava, cassava, etcetera.

I would be with my grandmother, sitting at her feet or standing beside her eagerly, waiting for the moment when she would nudge me and give me the okay to go pick out whatever fruit I wanted from what had been gathered. The merchants never argued or questioned me but would, in fact, assist me in selecting the best fruit(s) in the lot.

I also had the freedom to climb any of the trees and taste of and enjoy any fruits in season. No merchant or worker ever reprimanded me. They knew exactly who I was and to whom I belonged. My grandmother was the owner and I was one of the heirs. I, myself, had to be confident in that knowledge or I would never have attempted to eat of the fruits or vegetables of my grandparents' labor. How tragic it would have been had I lived in that orchard farm, starving and thinking I could not eat of those fruits because my grandfather was dead; or worse yet, that I had to have money to purchase anything I wanted on the farm.

I share this because before we get into the steps on how to operate in Gods provisions, you need to first identify yourself, know who you are or who you think you are, your thoughts about yourself and your life. You need to know, as God's child, where you have positioned yourself in Him. Are you on the inside enjoying your Father's benefits and blessings or are you on the outside, looking in?

Who Are You?

Excuse me if I come across bluntly and harshly, but here's the truth.

If you believe you are a no-good, going nowhere fast loser, then that is exactly who you are. If you think you always get the short end of the stick and nothing good ever comes your way, then that probably, is exactly what happens. You have allowed the enemy to come in, kill, steal, and destroy—to rob you of everything, your joy, peace and riches just as Jesus warned in John 10:10 that... *the thief comes only to steal and kill and destroy.*

If you are confident that God is on your side and He makes you prosper no matter what you do or where you go, then that is precisely who you are and probably, exactly what happens. God will cause you to prosper in every area of your life. He tells us again in John 10:10...*I came that they may have life, and have it abundantly.*

I know this because the Bible tells us in Proverbs 23:7 that whatever you think of yourself, how you perceive yourself, that is exactly who you are.

If you are like most people, you probably carry yourself the way you perceive yourself. Whether you believe it or not, and unless you are a great pretender, it comes out in your interactions with others on a daily basis, thereby transferring those perceptions to anyone who comes in contact with you, and they in turn conceive you as the person you have revealed to them.

For many years, secular books have instructed people to think, see and visualize themselves exactly where (what positions) they want to reach in life. People have obtained dramatic results and raved about these books, but what they fail to realize is that these principles originated from God and His word.

God's principles have been around since the beginning of time. God is the first to have spoken anything into existence. In the book of Genesis, God spoke the world exactly how He envisioned it.

Earlier in the chapter, I alluded to the question I am about to ask again.

How have you considered and positioned yourself? Not what others say about you, but who you think you are. Stop right now and give me three or four attributes you can say of your character. Would you describe yourself as insecure or confident, brave or fearful, shy, full of faith, a take charge person or a coward?

Who are you?

_____
_____
_____
_____
_____
_____

It is important for you to identify yourself in order to see if who you think you are matches up with who God created you to be. This will help you as you delve into His word and discover solutions for change. Your response to the above question provides the insight that will trigger the need for a paradigm shift. It will take you from negative to positive, from lack to abundance, from where you are, to catapulting you to levels above and beyond your expectations. This is what is needed in order for you to walk in God's blessings every day.

Right now, all we have are just your thoughts. It does not mean anything if we do not compare it with something. What we need to do is measure it against God's word. If your thoughts are not lining up with what God says in the Bible, then you need to look at ways to reshape and eradicate wrong thinking and ensue change.

In the next section, we will look at how to measure and pressure test your thoughts against God's thoughts for you.

Once you learn how to test your thinking, you can apply the method to any area of your life, spiritual, physical, emotional, mental, financial and otherwise.

If we establish that there is indeed alignment in your thinking with the Word of God, that's great. We pray that the scriptures outlined in this book will solidify your position in Christ even more. However, if we establish that there is misalignment with the Word of God and your way of thinking, what we will do then is provide the guidance for a fundamental change. Shifting your assumptions in the right way—the God way, will push you over into all the fullness of His glory. The end result and your gain will be victory over those areas where you need help, which is better than sitting on the fence, or worse, sitting off on the side of lack and failure.

In order to experience the kind of change/shifting I am talking about, you will have to get to the root cause of the problem to find out the why. However, when you discover and get to the root, you will need to uproot it (the old) and re-seed and re-build a new foundation.

> *Therefore if any man be in Christ, he is a*
> *new creature: old things are passed away;*
> *behold, all things are become new.*
> *2 Corinthians 5:17*

Before continuing, pause for a few minutes and think on these questions, and then pray for understanding as we move forward:

Are you happy at where you are now in your life? If not, why?

_____
_____
_____
_____
_____

Are you satisfied with the way things are going? If not, why?

_____
_____
_____
_____
_____

Who Are You?

What areas in your life could be improved?

_____
_____
_____
_____
_____

> *...that the God of our Lord Jesus Christ, the Father of glory, may give to you a spirit of wisdom and of revelation in the knowledge of Him.*
> *Ephesians 1:17*

Personal/Additional Notes:

_____
_____
_____
_____
_____
_____
_____
_____
_____
_____
_____
_____
_____

Personal/Additional Notes:

CHAPTER 5
Analyze Your Situation

And you will know the truth, and the truth will make you free.
John 8:32

The first and foremost step to a fundamental and positional change is to analyze your current situation, uncover the root problem and decipher how you got there in the first place.

Knowing the truth will set you free (John 8:32). It is that part of our foundation that enables us to build strong, steady pillars that define, shape and support us.

An unstable foundation cannot last long. It may appear solid at first, but when chipped at, it breaks because it is hollow inside. It crumbles due to factors like inferior building materials, diversion from the blue print, weather or environmental damage left untreated, and so much more.

There is a house in my neighborhood that I really love. Anyone who visits looks at it and marvels. Although it is not a brand-new building, it is a majestic, contemporary California-like mansion. So, you can imagine my excitement when the owners left and I had the opportunity to take a peek inside. While it still held its majestic ambience, it was falling apart and in terrible shape. All the things I could not see from afar became very evident up close. Part of the structure had settled on one end, making the building asymmetrical. Up close, I could see the outside walls had succumbed to weather damage because it had been left unattended.

Close examination revealed much more of the damage. It would require strengthening of the foundation, the walls, the roof and the entire structure all around to restore the house to its original glory.

The same actions would be required for you and me or any individual. A close inspection would be required to see the internal conditions and the repair and healing that would need to take place for a full restoration.

In order to fix your current situation, you need to closely examine your life. You must get answers to questions about your past and current situations in order to get all the way down to the bottom/the root of your disconnect, your lack, your behavior or illness and whatever is currently out of balance in your life. Through the help of the Holy Spirit, you can uncover the problem, and then develop and establish new ways of thinking for a blessed life.

You cannot devise a path for change if you do not know the underlying cause(s) as to why things are the way they are with you. In the same manner, a doctor cannot prescribe treatment for their patient without a diagnosis—without knowing exactly what is wrong.

A good doctor will use the process of deduction to eliminate any chance of a misdiagnosis. They ask questions, conduct exams; and to confirm any suspicions, they look for evidence via blood tests, x-rays, MRIs, and any other medical procedures that will show and reveal the root of the problem. Only from these deductions can a doctor rule out things they may have thought was present. This process of elimination provides the doctor an accurate identification of the nature of the illness so they can propose and prescribe the right treatment.

A lazy and uncaring physician may simply make an educated guess, dish out medication to mask the symptoms and cover the injury with a Band-Aid. That is not what we want.

So back to my question, how you are faring in your day-to-day activities? Are you high on top of the world, walking in the confidence that no matter which way you turn you are blessed? If you go east, west, north, or south, are you prosperous? If you travel domestically, internationally, or even intergalactically, do the blessings of God follow and overtake you no matter where you go?

Abraham lived, expecting to walk in God's blessings every day. In Genesis 13, Abraham and Lot were so prosperous that the land could no longer sustain them both. So, the decision was made for them to separate. Each needed to go his own way.

Abraham told Lot to decide, saying, "If you go to the left, I'll go to the right; if you go to the right, I'll go to the left." Abraham was so confident of his position in God, so sure that no matter what direction he took he would be blessed, that he gave first choice to Lot.

Can you confidently say that about your situation? That if someone had first choice, the pickings, the left overs would be far beyond your expectations?

Lot looked around and chose the most fertile ground, the plain of Jordan, toward the East. The Bible states that this portion of land, that Lot selected, looked just like the garden of the Lord because it was well watered. That's the one I would have chosen.

Abraham did not care. He was content with this, for he was confident at heart that he was blessed of God.

In Genesis 13, verses 14–17, Abraham's consideration of himself came to light. God called him to attention and told him to look to the North, South, East, and West. God said that all the land that Abraham was looking at, God was going to give to Abraham and his children. In addition, God promised to make Abraham's children innumerable—uncountable. If Abraham could count the stars in the sky, then that would be the number of his descendants.

On that note, let me ask you the following questions:

Are you physically well? Are your emotions in check? Are you of sound mind and spirit? Does the favor of God surround you so much so that you are in good standing with family and friends and on your job?

_____
_____
_____
_____
_____

Career wise and personally, are you at the top of your game? Are your bills met? Are you at peace with God and with yourself? Are you walking in the provisions God has made for His children?

_____
_____
_____
_____
_____

Are you drowning in the goodness of God?

_____
_____
_____
_____
_____

You might think it crazy that all those aspects in anyone's life can be in check all at one time, but that is the abundant life that Jesus offers us through His coming and

His death on the cross. We can obtain it when we align our thinking with God's thoughts of how He sees us.

While it is easy to provide our opinions about others, about our spouse, children, family members, neighbors, and people we work with, it is never an easy task taking a good look at ourselves and coming up with an honest answer. We are always in denial of who we really are. Whether we overemphasize ourselves as legends or as inferior to others, we lie to ourselves every day.

Since it is difficult to acknowledge our faults and weaknesses, we hide them deep in our subconscious. We choose to live in denial of these truths and continue in a negative, subpar existence that is contrary to God's word. These are the self-lies that I am talking about in this book.

If you are not satisfied with where you are in your life or where you are headed or why you are constantly struggling, there may be underlying reasons why. Whatever the root cause or stronghold, it needs to be dug up, dragged out and dealt with.

It could be a direct result of things or events that happened in your past, the environment you grew up in or even your current situation. These triggers, these happenings, may have rendered you powerless to fight for what rightfully belongs to you. We will dive more into these triggers, which I like to call blessing blockers, later on in the book.

You need to analyze your situation and deduce from the evidence why you are not operating in or receiving all of God's intended benefits and blessings. Being armed with that knowledge (your evidence) will assist in devising exactly how to treat and remove yourself from a position of lack and failure to a position of abundance and success.

As mentioned in the introduction, I have walked in the blessings of God and have also experienced the frustrations of assuming that the heavens were locked up with no access to my inheritance. I used the word "assuming" because the heavens are always open to God's children. We are the ones who put up walls, close the windows and barricade the doors to what God has for us. We are the ones who board up access to ourselves and assume God has closed the heavens to us.

Later on, I will explain how we as God's children close ourselves up from our Father's provisions by the things we do and fail to do. We refuse to confess the very words that our Heavenly Father has spoken over us, and yet, we allow others to confess and speak negative things into our lives. We allow their words to trap us in places God never intended for us to be, let alone get stuck in. We argue and bow our backs at God's words of redemption and stubbornly refuse to confess His words which He already pronounced over us, even when God, Himself, instructs us to do so. Yet, we willingly lay down in surrender to the enemy's plans as he runs amok in our lives, causing havoc in our ministries, our families, our jobs and communities.

If it appears that the devil's plans are in full operation in your life and it seems that you are not living the abundant life that Jesus describes in John 10:10, then it is time to do a reality check. This check measures how effective your life is that you confess to be living in His Name.

In a previous business, my husband and I had the responsibility of caring for the mentally ill. I learned a lot from my residents. One in particular, a well-educated, eloquent lady, who, when the enemy would bombard her with thoughts and fears that her son did not care for her, would relate the negative thoughts to me, and then ask me to do a reality check with her.

Reality check was to speak out loud the things her son had done for her: taking time out of his busy schedule not only to call and check on her, but to visit whenever he could (as he lived in another state); sending flowers for Mother's Day, calling to see how she was doing and sending her letters through the post. She would evaluate her son's actions against what she was hearing in her mind, against what the voices were telling her, and then deduce that the reality of it all was that she did have a son who cared for and loved her.

My resident had to know and receive the truth in order to dispel the lying thoughts in her head.

We as Christians need to do a reality check when the enemy bombards us with his lies and tells us that we are no good and that no one loves us.

When you hear negative words said against you and over you by family, friends, employers, co-workers, etc., what you need to do first and foremost, is to put a stop to

Analyze Your Situation

it. You need to stop people from confessing and speaking negative words over you; even in jesting. If you do not stop them, their words and their lies will creep into your heart and cause you to meditate on a mistruth until that mistruth becomes truth to you.

If God already declares that you are blessed, then, the truth is, my friend, you are blessed! No matter what anyone tells you. No matter what you see happening in your life.

You need to stand firm on God's truth. You have to believe and know in your heart that what your Father has said about you is the absolute truth. That is reality checking.

In the next section, you will examine your spiritual, emotional, mental, financial and other areas of your life against what God says about each area. Obtaining the result of that comparison is clue to knowing where you stand and to getting yourself back on track as God intended.

The exercises will require you to jot down your thoughts. So, if you need to, grab a pen or pencil before you continue. Find a place where you can be alone and not be distracted and situate yourself before going any further.

The check is really simple. You only need to do three things:
1. Review the scripture verse(s) and compare them against that respective area(s) in your life.
2. Write down the facts—how you are doing in this area, whether good, bad or indifferent.

3. Write down (be specific) what improvements you would like to see.

At the end of each short section is a grade to give you an idea of the position you have put yourself in Christ. There is no wrong answer whatsoever. The result is more of a compass to let you know where you are in your walk with God.

Put Me in remembrance, let us argue our case together;
State your cause, that you may be proved right.
Isaiah 43:26

Personal/Additional Notes:
_____
_____
_____
_____
_____
_____
_____
_____
_____
_____
_____
_____
_____

CHAPTER 6
Survey/Check Your Reality

But He was pierced for our transgressions, He was crushed for our iniquities; The chastening for our well-being fell upon Him, And by His scourging we are healed.
Isaiah 53:5

REALITY CHECK ON HEALING

We are about to discuss our thoughts and how we perceive the above scripture on healing. Let's find out how it's working for us. I'll do the first test with you, but do not skip over it. You need to derive your own answers to see how it applies to your life. My response is below. Enter yours in the blank lines provided.

What does Isaiah 53:5 mean to you?

Confidence that the sufferings/beatings Jesus endured on the cross was in exchange for anything that would happen to me; therefore, no sickness or disease can attack me and if and when they do, I have the assurance that Jesus paid the price so I can be healed.

Write your answer to the above question:

_____
_____
_____
_____
_____

If you are in need of healing, whether physical, mental, emotional or otherwise, does your life match up to God's intent of that scripture?

At the moment I am having a hard time holding on to this scripture because I have been struggling with sciatica nerve/back pain (it can be any sickness or disease) for almost two years (it can be any length of time). I have prayed, been prayed for and believed and claimed the promise of this scripture, explored all medical options and still continue to suffer. At times this is very discouraging.

Write your answer to the above question:

_____
_____
_____
_____
_____

Survey/Check Your Reality

How and what improvements would you like to see occur in the area of healing in your life?

Receive healing. As a child of God, I strongly believe that healing is part of my inheritance. I need to walk in divine health every day. Whatever the situation, whether sciatica, cancer, diabetes, headache, fever, I should receive that which has been paid for by Jesus.

Write your answer to the above question:
_____
_____
_____
_____
_____
_____

So, as you have seen in the above example, if healing is something you struggle with, then this is an area that you need to work on. Whether it is spiritual, emotional, mental, physical or financial healing, God's word dictates that because of the sacrifice Jesus made on the cross, you do not have to struggle with sickness or disease.

Healing belongs to you. What you need to do is collect those verses that outline God's promise for healing, and study them for application to your life. Your current situation and status should be in line with God's word.

Put a check mark on the line below for where you see yourself:

_____ Select 1-25% if you receive little or no healing encounters in your life

_____ Select 26-50% if you received healing on one or two occasions and/or the illness reoccurred

_____ Select 51-75% if you receive healing from time to time but not all the time

_____ Select 76-100% if you receive healing all or most of the time

As mentioned before, there is no right or wrong answer or perfect score or penalties. All the survey does is let you know what areas you need to work on.

If you scored between:
- 1-25% - There's a lot of work to be done to get you up to par.

- 26-50% - Although you have experienced some of what God intends for His children, there's still a lot of work to be done.

- 51-75% - You have experienced the promise and know it is true, but you need to keep working at it in order to stay in the constant flow of being blessed.

- 76-100% - You are on the right track and doing great. You know that God means you well and wants the best for you. Keep studying the word of God for the little push/encouragement to go all the way to walking in His promises daily.

Survey/Check Your Reality

You and I are not perfect, neither do the surveys in this book strive to take you to perfection. The aim/goal of each survey is to provide guidance and pinpoint your position in the different areas of your life when you measure your life to God's Word. The surveys are designed to show you where further study is required in order to get a grasp of God's truth and see it working to address your needs.

When you get that revelation, meditate upon it and stand on His word until you see the change God expects in your life.

It may be that you are doing excellent in the area of finances, but when it comes to healing, you doubt whether you have the faith to receive the healing you need. Be honest with yourself when doing these exercises. Discovering what you need to work on does not mean you neglect those areas where you are doing good. The goal is to restore and maintain wholeness and get you operating at full optimum power.

Please take each topic individually and work on them separately.

Now that you have seen an example of the survey, it is time for you to dig deep and do your own evaluation to see how you match up to what God has already declared of you.

REALITY CHECK ON SPIRITUAL PROMISE

Blessed be the God and Father of our Lord Jesus Christ, who has blessed us with every spiritual blessing in heavenly places in Christ.
Ephesians 1:3

Meditate on the above scripture. It infers that all the blessings that you will ever need, for any area of your life, have already been provided. Does that ring true in your life?

Write down what Ephesians 2:3 means to you.

_____
_____
_____
_____
_____
_____

Can you in confidence say you have received all provisions and benefits from God—all the blessings you ever need, in every area of your life?

_____
_____
_____
_____
_____

Survey/Check Your Reality

What spiritual improvements would you like to see and in what area of your life?

_____
_____
_____
_____
_____
_____

Put a check mark on the line below for where you see yourself:

_____ Select 1-25% if you receive little to no provision or blessings from God
_____ Select 26-50% if you receive or have received some sort of provision or benefit but have not received fully as the scripture indicates
_____ Select 51-75% if you receive His blessings from time to time but not all the time
_____ Select 76-100% if you receive and walk in His blessings most of the time

REALITY CHECK ON EMOTIONAL AND MENTAL PROMISE

For God did not give us a spirit of timidity or cowardice or fear, but [He has given us a spirit] of power and of love and of sound judgment and personal discipline [abilities that result in a calm, well-balanced mind and self-control].
2 Timothy 1:7 (AMP)

God provides peace for us. He assures us that fear does not originate from Him and that we should walk in His love and in soundness of mind.

Write down what 2 Timothy 1:7 on emotional and mental healing means to you.

_____
_____
_____
_____
_____

Do you walk in soundness of mind and do you have the peace that God gives or are you overwhelmed with fear and confusion?

_____
_____
_____
_____
_____
_____

If you are not operating in the provisions of 2 Timothy 1:7, what would you like to see occur in this area of your life?

_____
_____
_____
_____

Survey/Check Your Reality

_____
_____

Put a check mark on the line below for where you see yourself:

_____ Select 1-25% if you are constantly troubled and cannot find peace of mind

_____ Select 26-50% if you do receive peace of mind but the times are few and far between

_____ Select 51-75% if you receive peace of mind from time to time but not all the time

_____ Select 76-100% if you walk in peace and soundness of mind most of the time

REALITY CHECK ON FINANCIAL PROMISE

And my God will supply all your needs according to His riches in glory in Christ Jesus.
Philippians 4:19

God delights in seeing that all your needs are met and has made all the provisions necessary for you to live debt free. His very name, Jehovah Jireh, literally means God the Provider. That is exactly what God does for you and me. He provides all our needs (and not just financially).

What do you think Philippians 4:19 means? Does it apply to you as a child of God?

_____
_____
_____
_____
_____
_____

Are your needs met? Are you living from paycheck to paycheck and receiving just enough to cover your bills, or are you living in the overflow? In what other areas do you have a need or lack?

_____
_____
_____
_____
_____
_____

How and what improvements would you like to see occur in this area of your life?

_____
_____
_____
_____
_____
_____

Survey/Check Your Reality

Put a check mark on the line below for where you see yourself:

_____ Select 1-25% if you receive little or no financial blessing or prosperity
_____ Select 26-50% if you receive/have received some financial blessing or prosperity but not fully
_____ Select 51-75% if you receive and experience financial blessing or prosperity from time to time but not all the time
_____ Select 76-100% if you receive financial blessing/prosperity most of the time

REALITY CHECK ON FAITH

> *Truly I say to you, whoever says to this mountain, 'Be taken up and cast into the sea,' and does not doubt in his heart, but believes that what he says is going to happen, it will be granted him.*
> *Mark 11:23*

What does Mark 11:23 mean to you?

_____
_____
_____
_____
_____
_____

Do you have faith to withstand your current situation? Do you have the faith to believe that

things will change as you apply God's word and His principles to your life?

_____
_____
_____
_____
_____

The Bible says that all you need is faith as small as a mustard seed. Do you have that much faith? If not, how and what improvements would you like to see occur in this area of your life?

_____
_____
_____
_____
_____
_____

Put a check mark on the line below for where you see yourself:
_____ Select 1-25% if you operate in little or no faith with no results at all
_____ Select 26-50% if you operate in some faith some of the time with little or no results
_____ Select 51-75% if you operate in faith some of the time with some results
_____ Select 76-100% if you operate in faith most of the time with 75% or more results

REALITY CHECK ON DIVINE PROTECTION

He who dwells in the shelter of the Most High Will abide in the shadow of the Almighty. 2 I will say to the Lord, "My refuge and my fortress, My God, in whom I trust!" 3 For it is He who delivers you from the snare of the trapper And from the deadly pestilence. 4 He will cover you with His pinions, And under His wings you may seek refuge; His faithfulness is a shield and bulwark. Psalm 91:1-4

What does Psalm 91 on God's protection mean to you?

_____
_____
_____
_____
_____

Are there areas in your life where you feel unprotected (it could be over you, your spouse, children, business)?

_____
_____
_____
_____

What protection would you like to see occur, in what area, and for whom (family member) are you seeking covering for?

_____
_____
_____
_____
_____
_____

Put a check mark on the line below for where you see yourself:

_____ Select 1-25% if you received little or no protection at all

_____ Select 26-50% if you receive some sort of protection but not full covering

_____ Select 51-75% if you receive/have received Godly protection from time to time but not all the time

_____ Select 76-100% if you receive Godly protection 75% or more of the time

You can see from the scriptures given that God promises and expects you to prosper in all areas of your life. In fact, above and beyond all that you can ask or think.

Feel free to pressure test your favorite scriptures and other scriptures to see how they are working for you against how God intended for them to be applied in your life.

Survey/Check Your Reality

Personal/Additional Notes:

Personal/Additional Notes:

CHAPTER 7
Uncover Your Roots

Search me, O God, and know my heart; Try me and know my anxious thoughts; And see if there be any hurtful way in me, And lead me in the everlasting way.
Psalm 139:23-24

Your thoughts, your character and how you react to triggers in your life are rooted in an acquired concept or belief. This may have been derived through environmental, cultural, familial or a number of different stimulants.

Whichever way you acquired and adopted your thinking and reactions to things is the result of past failures and successes. These responses have shaped and molded you to who you are today.

Your thoughts, who you think you are and what you believe, determine whether you live your life in fear or in boldness, in defeat or in victory.

Getting to the root cause is pivotal to knowing why you are where you are today and exactly where you will end up tomorrow and every day thereafter, unless there is change.

Once you see yourself for who you really are, the next thing is to find out why things are the way they are in your life.

There is no sense in saying you have arrived at a position without knowing how you got there. It is like seeing a great performer at a concert who once played in the subways or, better yet, a CEO who is now homeless. In each situation, you cannot help but wonder what happened that landed both performer and CEO in their current positions; from rags to riches or from riches to rags.

No one is without a past. No matter how chaotic or humdrum your life is at present, your past holds the keys to everything you are today and will be in the future. Probing the past (and scrutinizing the present) is what this book is all about, requiring you to dig deep into the past so you can find and eradicate the root of the problem.

Probing exposes the portals in your life. The enemy is always looking for cracks in our foundations, our structures and any open doors through which he can sneak in and cause havoc. The Bible compares this concept to little foxes that spoil the vineyard (Song of Solomon 2:15 *Catch the foxes for us, The little foxes that are ruining the vineyards, While our vineyards are in blossom*).

The root cause of your current demise could be something that happened to you as a child or an adult that wounded your heart and penetrated deep into your soul, causing hurt, mistrust, low self-esteem, doubt and a number of negative results.

The events in your past have worked to shape your today. They have landed you right where you are and are probably keeping you bound and stuck. How you handle the circumstances you face now will shape and direct where you find yourself tomorrow.

This is why it is imperative that you learn how to handle things the right way—the God way. All activities/events from this point forward should lead to an assurance of a prosperous life and future and ensure an expected end as God has declared in Jeremiah 29:11.

Our Heavenly Father has given us explicit guidelines, in the Bible, on how to live a prosperous life. God desires above all things that you prosper and be in good health even as your soul prospers (3 John 1:2-5).

Your soul encompasses all that you are, which consists of the different components such as spiritual, physical, emotional, mental, financial, as well as peace and security (divine protection). Think of each component as a different piece of a puzzle. When all these pieces are put together, they make a beautiful picture—YOU. And more so, specifically, the you God designed.

When any of these pieces become misaligned, damaged or misplaced over time due to life events/triggers, it impacts the prosperity of the body, the mind, the soul, and spirit.

You need to take time out and ask God to reveal to you the causes and events (past or present) that have affected your considerations of yourself and your state of being.

Whether it is rejection, a loss, abuse (verbal, emotional, physical, and/or sexual) from others, it needs to be dealt with so that you can move on in God.

Whatever it is that God reveals to you, bring it under His divine light, and immerse it in the precious blood of Jesus and pray for God's healing.

> *Be of sober spirit, be on the alert. Your adversary, the devil, prowls around like a roaring lion, seeking someone to devour.*
> *1 Peter 5:8*

Personal/Additional Notes:

_____
_____
_____
_____
_____
_____
_____
_____
_____
_____
_____
_____
_____
_____

CHAPTER 8
Identify Blessing Blockers

²⁹ Let no unwholesome word proceed from your mouth, but only such a word as is good for edification according to the need of the moment, so that it will give grace to those who hear. ³⁰ Do not grieve the Holy Spirit of God, by whom you were sealed for the day of redemption. ³¹ Let all bitterness and wrath and anger and clamor and slander be put away from you, along with all malice. ³² Be kind to one another, tender-hearted, forgiving each other, just as God in Christ also has forgiven you.
Ephesians 4:29-32

As mentioned before, like any good doctor, psychologist or detective would do to find out what ails their patient or solve a crime, you must be willing to examine your past and present. Only by so doing will you be able to deduce the problem, come up with an accurate diagnosis, and then provide treatment or solution.

You will also understand the why of your lack, your failures, your inadequacies and anything that is contrary to God's plan in your life.

Let me warn you that this part of the process can be painful. As you search deep and dig up events that occurred up to this point, some things you uncover and face may not be pleasant at all. You may even say that you cannot recall any fun memories from your childhood or past marriage or relationships. You may have buried them (events and the painful memories) deep in your subconscious because these memories are painful; yet, just because you have suppressed them does not mean they do not have a cause and effect relationship in your life.

Here are a couple of questions for you to ponder:

What event from your past or present situation do you believe has been or is a showstopper for you. That event, that point, after which, things changed in your life?

_____

_____

_____

What is it about your current lifestyle that has you stuck in a rut and inhibits you from being whole and walking in the power and glory of God?

_____

_____

_____

Identify Blessing Blockers

Are there hidden secrets that torment and paralyze you from being free and stepping out and being your true self?

_____

_____

_____

Are your persuasions the result of childhood experiences, your environment, an abusive past or current relationship(s)?

_____

_____

_____

Could it be that you have maneuvered the course of your life and landed exactly where you are because you consistently line up your words with negative prognosis and the lies of others?

Allow me to repeat something I said in an earlier chapter. If you do not attack the lies that come at you (whether in your mind or from people around you), those lies will creep into your heart and cause you to meditate on a mistruth until it becomes a part of you and your truth.

You must know by now that these words from other people are contrary to how God sees you and what He wants for you.

Perhaps your situation is different. Perhaps you used to walk in the blessings of God, but now it seems that you have fallen out of favor with God and those around you.

Perhaps the priorities and distractions in your life are pulling you down; drawing you to places and situations unfamiliar to you, circumstances you know are not conducive to abundant life. People, things, and places you would never have tolerated before.

How do you back pedal out of it all?

As I mentioned in the Analyze Your Situation chapter, it is not my intention to cause you grief or pain. But if things are not going right and you have to go fishing and stir up murky waters to find out what and where the blockage in the pipe is, trust me, it will be worth the peace and freedom you achieve in the long run. It will be worth your expected end, which includes receipt of all the benefits and blessings you will ever need while walking on this earth.

You need to take control, take charge and be ready to rid yourself of all stinking thinking.

Dare to be a Daniel or a Moses or a Joshua. Dare to be an Esther or a Ruth. Dare to be different. Dare to be in sync with God from this moment forward, no matter who likes it or not.

Take, for example, a runner who suddenly gets a dirty, rusty nail in his foot. He cannot walk or run. He is aware the reason is because of that nail stuck in his foot. He knows it's going to hurt to try to remove it, but even so, he knows that in order for him to resume his normal activities, that nail needs to come out. He would never be complacent leaving the nail to fester, if he knows what's good for him. It could cost him his foot and even his life.

Identify Blessing Blockers

This is serious business. Set apart some quiet and alone time with God. If you need to, grab a pen and notebook. Get ready to write down all that the Holy Spirit brings to your remembrance.

In your quiet time, I want you to ask God to reveal to you the various events/triggers that have altered and shaped your way of thinking. What is it that has landed you in the position you are now in, today?

The goal is to uncover the cracks in the foundation. Let us learn together what things and actions are wrong so that we can fix them by using God's instructions. It is by so doing that you will get back on God's track for your life.

In the book, *Absolute Surrender,* by Andrew Murray, he describes our lives as a train on a track. When and if that train gets derailed, his recommendation is to go back to the shunt. The shunt is that point or position on the train's forward track and path where it derails and takes a turn, and then goes in a totally different direction. One definition of shunting is to push or shove someone or something. Another definition describes shunting as the act of directing or diverting someone or something to a lesser/unfavorable position.

When we get shunted off of God's path for our lives, we need to go back to that point where things started going awry; back to the place where we were last in sync with God before we got diverted to a lesser or unfavorable position. Hence the reason for the questions asked earlier in this chapter. They served to prompt you to think back and identify those events which started your life spiraling down the wrong path.

So, let us get to the nitty-gritty of things. Enter into your travel capsule, press the year, bring up whatever incidents that register with you as we go through this section to uncover events that have wrongly impacted your life and prevented you from soaring to higher heights. Some of us don't even have to think about it. We know that exact point, exact day and time when things started going wrong.

Was it after the death of a parent, spouse, someone close, a loved one? Could it have been an illness or event that left you resentful and incapable of fulfilling your dreams? Do you feel God and others have rejected you? Perhaps it was disobedience to God, a parent or spouse, angry words spat out at you during an altercation with a spouse, friend, co-worker? Do you still hold unforgiveness, anger or hate because of that person or event?

Write down your answer. My questions are simply prompts to jar and loosen hidden, suppressed and forgotten memories in order to get to the root.

_____
_____
_____
_____
_____

Perhaps it was the moment you allowed a certain person (or people) in your life. It could be a church or business venture you entered into and ignored all your inner/heart

Identify Blessing Blockers

warnings. Toxic relationships, toxic environments, toxic decisions can all lead to drastic and detrimental changes in our lives. Do not think it crazy or foolish, but there are some people whose entrance in our lives bring nothing but grief, hardship, pain and destruction. There are others though who come as supporters and helpers and who lift us up and empower us on our journey.

Ask the Holy Spirit to assist you as you demystify the dynamics of past and current relationships. It may be between you and your parents or other family members, or platonic or intimate relationships.

_____
_____
_____
_____
_____

Write down the names of people or places you sense or have always felt a conviction to separate yourself from. Places you have no business visiting. Ask God's forgiveness for not obeying that inner prompting. His Holy Spirit will impart to you the strength you need to remove yourself from that situation.

_____
_____
_____
_____
_____
_____

What I want you to do now is to dig a little deeper to expose those barriers and pull down those strongholds that block the blessings from coming through to you. I call these blessing blockers, and I want to touch on them, as it is important to know and address them in order for healing to be effective.

When studying the word of God, if you come across a promise of God that you feel is not happening or evident in your life, be encouraged, stay in the Word and pray it through. Perform a reality check as you did in Chapter 6 and check the reality of your situation against that scripture. Always ask God to show you what you need to do to ensue change.

If, for example, you read in Nahum 1:9 that affliction will not rise up a second time, but find yourself struggling with a recurring habit, addiction or sickness, keep standing on the scripture and believing until you see the truth of God's spoken word come to pass—until that sickness or addiction never attacks you again.

UNCONFESSED SIN

Anyone who has either attended a Catholic Church or school knows the importance of going to confession. It is, for me, one of the most valuable acts I learned in Catholic school. This is something I believe the Christian Church fails to talk about and encourage. I know Jesus tore the veil through His death on the cross, thereby giving us direct access to our Heavenly Father. For this reason, we don't need to confess to a priest, per se, but the Bible does encourage us to confess our sins one to another (even if it happens to be a priest, especially the person we have wronged) and pray for one another so that we, ourselves, will receive healing (James 5:16).

I think that we, as Christians, should make a conscious effort to come to God daily and confess our sins. It is an act of cleansing that is vital to prosperity in Christ. No matter how perfect you may think you are, we hurt others and we disobey God in our thoughts, the things we do, fail to do, the words we speak, and our refusal to follow the basic things He has asked us to do in the Bible and in His commandments. We have all sinned and fallen short of God's Glory (Romans 3:23-26).

Sin separates us from God. Daily confession delivers us and keeps us free from encumbrances that hinder our blessings from coming through. Sin is the number one blessing blocker. It opens the door for the enemy to come into our lives and create havoc. Unconfessed sin negates the power of our prayers. Yet, God has not left us without hope. He states in 1 John 1:9 that *if we confess our sins, He (God) is faithful and just to forgive us and cleanse us from all unrighteousness.*

We thank God for the power contained in the Blood of Jesus, which cleanses us not only from our sins but also renders us righteous in God (2 Corinthians 5:21 *He made Him who knew no sin to be sin on our behalf, so that we might become the righteousness of God in Him*).

It is through this transfer of righteousness through Jesus' Blood that we have been given the boldness to enter into God's presence (Hebrews 4:16, Ephesians 3:12).

I pray that in your quiet time that the Holy Spirit reveals to you whatever lurks deep in your heart and in your past that keeps you bound. Ask God to help you forgive those who have wronged you so that you do not harbor any hard feelings toward them. Be willing to forgive just as God through Christ forgave you.

Forgive yourself also if there is something you did in your past that keeps coming up and binding you from moving forward in God. If you confess your sins, God will forgive you and He will remove them (your sins) as far as the East is from the West. He remembers them (your sins) no more.

In today's world, we hear so much, see so much and get involved in things that grieve the Holy Spirit whether we want to or not. This is because we are surrounded by so much filth and immorality blasting at us every second of the day, and everywhere we turn. It is for this reason I urge you to do a daily prayer for cleansing of the defilements of each day before you go to bed.

Write down your own personal prayer of confession. Ask the Holy Spirit to direct you.

YOUR TONGUE

Believe it or not, another damaging blessing blocker is the tongue. It is no wonder that there are many scriptures that warn us about its power. Proverbs 13:3 tells us that *...he that keepeth his mouth keepeth his life: but he that openeth wide his lips shall have destruction.* It literally means that we have to watch over the words we speak if we want to live life the way God intended.

An effort and desire for change starts by checking your thoughts and guarding what comes out of your mouth. This also means being careful not to gripe and complain or gossip or slander others with our words. There are consequences when we do these things. It cost the Israelites 40 years in the wilderness to make a journey that would have taken them 40 days, simply because of their complaining.

As creatures of habit, lovers of idioms and clichés, we utter phrases so lightly, so flippantly, not really grasping that our words are so powerful that they can span generations. It is not only your life that is at stake and that you affect when you speak and confess these negative sayings, but your children's lives also for generations to come. Instead of saying that the job or your kids will be your death, or that something is killing you, that nothing good or no one great ever comes from your family line, that your son or daughter will never amount to anything because of their current behavior, how about confessing God's promises over your life and that of your children's and your loved ones?

During my college years, I had convinced myself that come September, just as soon as classes started, I would get sick as a dog with the flu. I was very confident of that fact. I expected it and prepared for it because it occurred without fail, year-after-year.

You probably see where I'm going.

I dreaded it, but at the same time, I could not figure out why it was happening religiously, every year, until I realized that my body was executing/manifesting and obeying the words I had spoken over it for years. Once I caught onto that, I stopped speaking sickness over my body, and guess what? I stopped getting sick every September, and no, I do not take flu shots. I curbed my tongue. I learned to set a watch over my mouth. The moment I feel attacked in my body or my mind or spirit, I immediately begin to confess God's word. Sometimes it is not easy, but I persevere through it.

So, am I perfect in every aspect of my life? No. I am learning to overcome stubborn areas by speaking what God has already spoken over the situations that come up, no matter whether it is physical, spiritual, emotional or mental. My sword is in my mouth. I fight my battles with God's words.

It is not just the words you speak, but also those thoughts you think and never utter. Your thoughts are unspoken, unrevealed words, but they are words in your mind. So, if you are thinking that you don't speak like that, but yet in your mind you think that way, then you have to curb those thoughts as well, as they too will keep you stuck right where you are.

Identify Blessing Blockers

James 3:4-14 warrants a place here:

4 And a small rudder makes a huge ship turn wherever the pilot chooses to go, even though the winds are strong. 5 In the same way, the tongue is a small thing that makes grand speeches. But a tiny spark can set a great forest on fire. 6 And among all the parts of the body, the tongue is a flame of fire. It is a whole world of wickedness, corrupting your entire body. It can set your whole life on fire, for it is set on fire by hell itself. 7 People can tame all kinds of animals, birds, reptiles, and fish, 8 but no one can tame the tongue. It is restless and evil, full of deadly poison. 9 Sometimes it praises our Lord and Father, and sometimes it curses those who have been made in the image of God. 10 And so blessing and cursing come pouring out of the same mouth. Surely, my brothers and sisters, this is not right! 11 Does a spring of water bubble out with both fresh water and bitter water? 12 Does a fig tree produce olives, or a grapevine produce figs? No, and you can't draw fresh water from a salty spring. 13 If you are wise and understand God's ways, prove it by living an honorable life, doing good works with the humility that comes from wisdom. 14 But if you are bitterly jealous and there is selfish ambition in your heart, don't cover up the truth with boasting and lying.
James 3:4-14 (NLT)

Unfortunately, not only do we need to watch over the words we speak, but we also need to guard what comes in through our mouth. In some cases, divine health has no spiritual bearing but that we need to watch our food intake. If we eat healthy, we stay healthy; if we eat badly, we open ourselves up for a not-so-good physical state. Watch what goes in and watch what comes out.

Let's get serious here. It is so important that you put a guard over your mouth. The words that you speak over your life and the lives of your loved ones will determine your destiny and theirs also—where you and they will end up. Think about that for a moment. Think of your parents, your son or daughter, your husband or wife and their careers and goals. Think about God's destiny for all your lives and what would happen and how you would feel if because of the negative words you speak, you redirected their paths and yours to the opposite end of where God intended for each of you to land?

You, through your words negated and shunted God's destiny for all or your lives.

You are the driver, the navigator, you control the GPS. Whatever coordinates you set in the GPS by your thoughts and words, is the location you and your loved ones will end up—either in the "Life is Good Highway" or the "Life Sucks Lane."

The negative words that you speak overrides God's destiny—God's good purpose that has already been set in motion. Your words have the power to literally change the trajectory of God's plan for your life or propel it in the direction God already intended.

Which will you choose? These next two scriptures below provide not only the clue, but the answer.

> *Death and life are in the power of the tongue,*
> *And those who love it will eat its fruit.*
> *Proverbs 18:21*

> *I call heaven and earth to witnesses against you today, that I have set before you life and death, the blessing and the curse. So choose life in order that you may live, you and your descendants.*
> *Deuteronomy 30:19*

Out of everything I have to say, this is the most powerful, the most effective lesson that you can take away from this book, bar none. Speaking God's words over your life will bring you such abundance that it will exceed far above and beyond what you could have ever imagined or expected. As you go through this book or your daily devotionals, write down scriptures you read of God's promises and begin to confess them over your life and that of your loved ones. Date the start of your confessions, and then revisit and evaluate your position six months or a year later to see your position.

DISOBEDIENCE

God gave the 10 Commandments, a summary of His laws. Then He put that and the remainder of His instructions, as guidelines in the Bible on how we should live our lives.

We put ourselves in unnecessary pain and hardship when we do not obey His laws. Yes, we are under His grace, but that does not give us the license to be reckless in life. The Bible holds mathematical equations for our lives. It contains formulas and conditional statements where God gives the instructions for having an abundant life. Most people do not like to think the Bible is formulaic, but it is.

Don't believe?

- Want eternal life? Confess your sins and ask Jesus into your heart as your Lord and Savior. John 3:16
- Want long life? Honor your parents so that it will be well with you. Exodus 20:12
- Want prosperity? Stop stealing from God and start paying your tithes. Malachi 3:10
- Want God to exalt you? Obey His commandments. Deuteronomy 28:1
- Want others to be kind to you and show you favor? Treat them the way you want to be treated. Luke 3:16, Ephesians 4:32
- Want to find God? Seek Him with all your heart. Deuteronomy 4:29, Proverbs 8:17, Matthew 7:7

The above are just a handful of formulas in the Bible; "if you do this, then this will happen".

Check out the entire chapter of Deuteronomy 28. It sheds light on how our obedience and disobedience can lead to blessings or curses that effect an entire generation. This is why it is important to study the word of God and be acquainted with your Heavenly Father. Do not trust others to tell you what your Heavenly Father is like. Spend time with Him and He will reveal Himself to you.

Then [with a deep longing] you will seek Me and require Me [as a vital necessity] and [you will] find Me when you search for Me with all your heart.
Jeremiah 29:13 (AMP)

OTHER BLESSING BLOCKERS

There are many other blessing blockers besides your tongue, unconfessed sin, unforgiveness and disobedience. One, or any combination, of the blessing blockers we have already discussed and the ones listed below may be preventing you from walking in God's provisions.

When not dealt with, blessing blockers become strongholds that lock us down, paralyze us from moving from point A to point B. They can be triggered by others, ourselves or our environments. Whatever the cause, however it presents itself, a blessing blocker or stronghold cannot and must not have a place in your life.

The list of blessing blockers below is in no particular order. As you go through them, pause for a moment and let the Holy Spirit reveal to you events from your past or present that trigger these emotions. I have combined some of them as they are closely related in meaning and relation.

Write your thoughts on any incident(s) that comes to mind in the lines provided. Remember, this is for your eyes only.

REJECTION / FEAR / UNREQUITED LOVE / ABANDONMENT LONELINESS / SELF-PITY / SADNESS

Do you feel rejected by a parent, spouse, friends, or a loved one, or were you passed over for a promotion? Did someone give up on or abandon you, left you when you needed them most?

_____
_____
_____
_____

UNFORGIVENESS / NOT WALKING IN LOVE / HATE / MALICE / ANGER TOWARD GOD AND OTHERS

Have the actions of others left you bitter and hateful and unwilling to forgive or trust or give your heart to others? Are you angry at God for things that happened in the past or present? Who is/was it and what was the incident?

_____
_____
_____
_____

TOXIC RELATIONSHIPS / TOXIC ENVIRONMENTS / DESTRUCTIVE EMOTIONS & DECISIONS

People who degrade you and abuse you verbally, mentally, physically or sexually cause toxic relationships and toxic environments. Destructive emotions can be the result of toxic relationships and environments, which in turn cause you to make bad decisions because of the fear and control of someone else. Toxic relationships and environments and destructive emotions are detrimental in many ways. They can be more difficult to break simply because you become dependent on the very habits and people and environments that you need to separate yourself from.

This could be your home, especially when children are involved, your workplace, a controlling church, an abusive or immoral relationship where you need to break the soul ties that have been formed. Even though these relationships are all toxic, you stick around because, in your mind, you need these people and can associate with their behavior or place, and it feels familiar and comfortable to you.

There is no shame or condemnation in coming to terms with the fact that you need professional help in order to break free. In fact, I encourage you to find good Christian counseling that provides a safe environment for you to share and receive guidance. Ask the Holy Spirit for direction and the strength to do what needs to be done.

INHERITED / GENERATIONAL CURSES

You are not at fault here. Inherited/generational curses are tied to your family line and DNA because of something an ancestor or parent did or failed to do or put into motion by their words or actions. The results got passed down through the generations. You know it by the same illness or addiction (drinking, double-mindedness, schizophrenia, lack of finances, progress, etc.,) occurring generation after generation in your blood line.

This brings me to the point I made earlier, that the coordinates you put in the GPS with your mouth not only affects you, but it gets passed down to your children and their children for generations. What are some things that come to mind that you see occurring in your family line?

LIES / JEALOUSY / GOSSIP / COMPLAINING / NEGATIVE WORDS & THOUGHTS

These all line up with the section on the tongue. What areas of your speech do you need to line up with God's word or what habit do you need to break? Do you find yourself talking about others, coworkers, the pastor, brothers and sisters at the Church? If so, ask God's forgiveness now.

_____
_____
_____
_____
_____
_____
_____

DISBELIEF / FALSE TEACHINGS & HERESIES / UNANSWERED PRAYERS

Confess and repent of your disbelief and any false teachings you may have received. Praying about something once or throwing up a Hail Mary does not constitute prayer. It is coming to God daily, being persistent, getting a hold of God until that answer manifests in this realm. Trust God to answer your prayers.

_____
_____
_____
_____

I would urge you to deal with any of the above-mentioned blessing blockers that the Holy Spirit assists you in identifying so that you can move on and upward in your life.

If you are harboring unforgiveness or hate toward someone, a parent, past love, friend or teacher, I urge you to forgive those people and let it go. It is not worth the self-torment which you put yourself through nor the physical illness or mental stress that results from living with these negative emotions.

Being angry or unforgiving causes wounds and illnesses to fester inside you. I agree with the adage that harboring anger, hate, unforgiveness and all these toxic emotions is like drinking poison and expecting the other person to die. Forgiveness is not just for the other person but for you, so that you can fly free, without any encumbrances.

The Bible urges us in Romans 12:18, that, *if at all possible, as far as it depends on you, live at peace with everyone.* This was my mother's motto for life.

We have a saying in my hometown of Freetown, that the enemy looks for where there is peace in order to bring strife and contention. Why? Simply because strife and contention do not bring about the righteousness of God nor allow you to walk in health and love and in God's provisions.

I urge you once again to meditate on God's word. Ask the Holy Spirit for revelation, and then examine your own life against that scripture. If your life does not measure up to the standards God has expressed in His Word/the Bible, then you need to pray and ask the Holy Spirit for the discipline and strength you need to be obedient to God, to bridle your tongue, to speak blessings over your life and to breathe life into the very words you speak.

Here are some guidelines for you:

1. Make God a partner in your day-to-day activities.

2. Allow the Holy Spirit to be a catalyst, the fire-burning element you need, to get things moving.

3. Know and acknowledge that you do not need to strive for/work out your salvation. Why? Jesus already did the work on the cross for you. All you need to do is to speak the very words Jesus spoke and call things into being just like Jesus did.

4. Speak over your life. Speak exactly what God has spoken over you as His child, and what you want to see happening for you, your spouse, your children, your ministry, your business, and your community, in accordance with God's word.

You can do this!

12 What man is he that desireth life, and loveth many days, that he may see good? 13 Keep thy tongue from evil, and thy lips from speaking guile.14 Depart from evil, and do good; seek peace, and pursue it.
Psalm 34:13-14

Personal/Additional Notes:

CHAPTER 9
Pull Down Strongholds

4 for the weapons of our warfare are not of the flesh, but divinely powerful for the destruction of fortresses.
2 Corinthians 10:4

You may think to yourself that you are not a fighter nor the right person to go into battle; but I am here to tell you that you are well equipped for spiritual warfare.

Your Heavenly Father knows that your fight is not carnal, it is not a fight of your wits or of your flesh as stated in 2 Corinthians 10:4. We cannot use man-made artillery when we go into spiritual battle with the enemy or we will not be able to pull down strongholds.

Strongholds are those blessing blockers, that have not been dealt with and are left to take root in your life. Strongholds are chains, fetters that have you bound and that render you incapable of being the you God designed.

As we have seen in earlier chapters these strongholds/blessing blockers could be physical, spiritual, or a pattern of behavior. They paralyze you and hold you captive; a prisoner in your own mind, your body, your soul and your spirit

Indeed our war is spiritual but God provided an armor of protection for you for the battle. It is in Ephesians chapter 6:14-17.

Verses 11 and 12 admonishes you to... 11 *Put on the full armor of God, so that you will be able to stand firm against the schemes of the devil. 12 For our struggle is not against flesh and blood, but against the rulers, against the powers, against the world forces of this darkness, against the spiritual forces of wickedness in the heavenly places.*

Whatever it is, do not be discouraged.

David knew the Lord was with Israel and with him when he faced Goliath. Rest assured that God is with you now and always. The victory has already been won. You are merely going in to collect the spoils and your possessions just as David did.

The Amalekites had raided the Israelites' camp and taken the wives and children of David and his men. The men were angry, the Bible tells us, but instead of giving into the anger, David strengthened himself in God, and asked God what he should do. David did not ask the men or his friends what they thought. David sought God for the answer.

God then gave David the green light to go and get what the enemy had stolen from him. David did, and this is the report; notice in verse 20 that he, David, got back more than the enemy had plundered.

18 So David recovered all that the Amalekites had taken, and rescued his two wives. 19 Nothing of theirs was missing whether small or great, sons or daughters, spoil or anything that had been taken; David recovered it all. 20 So David captured all the flocks and herds [which the enemy had], and [the people] drove those animals before him and said, "This is David's spoil."
1 Samuel 30:18-20

Jesus already won the battle for you when he died on the cross. He exposed the enemy's evil plots and plans, destroying them once and for all. It is time to strengthen yourself in your God, and go and get back all the enemy has stolen from you.

Years ago, I reconnected with a friend after about a decade. I was surprised that she was still single. She is gorgeous, well dressed and a hard worker who always had a strong desire to be married. In our group of friends, I thought she would have been the first to be married. I could not figure out what the problem was until she told me one day of an incident that happened when she was about sixteen. She had chosen to go to the movies with friends rather than to the weekday Church service. Her pastor at the time, in his anger, spoke some terrible words over her and declared that she would never marry but end up an old maid.

How tragic that those who are responsible for guiding the flock get mad and speak evil over their sheep. I tried to explain to my friend that she needed to rebuke those words, bring that pastor's evil declarations under the Blood of Jesus and break their power and stronghold over her, regardless of the length of time since the incident.

Rather than allow those words to take root in her life, she needs to reclaim that joy of being a wife and a mother that was stolen from her. Unfortunately, only she can make that happen.

For a paradigm shift to occur, you will need to take a stand over those blessing blockers and strongholds you identified in Chapter 8. God has given you the power and authority, through the Blood of Jesus Christ, to break the chains of the enemy and tear down strongholds.

Put on your armor therefore! It is time to go in and recover and repossess your possessions.

14 Stand firm therefore, having girded your loins with truth, and having put on the breastplate of righteousness, 15 and having shod your feet with the preparation of the gospel of peace; 16 in addition to all, taking up the shield of faith with which you will be able to extinguish all the flaming arrows of the evil one. 17 And take the helmet of salvation, and the sword of the Spirit, which is the word of God.
Ephesians 6:14-17

CHAPTER 10
God Has Regarded You

16 For God so loved the world, that he gave his only begotten Son, that whosoever believeth in him should not perish, but have everlasting life.
John 3:16

For I know the thoughts that I think toward you, saith the Lord, thoughts of peace, and not of evil, to give you an expected end.
Jeremiah 29:11

17 How precious also are thy thoughts unto me, O God! how great is the sum of them! 18 If I should count them, they are more in number than the sand: when I awake,
I am still with thee.
Psalm 139:17-18

2 Beloved, I wish above all things that thou mayest prosper and be in health, even as thy soul prospereth.
3 John 1:2

There are many scriptures that tell how much God loves you and how fondly He thinks of you. The above are a few of my favorite. I encourage you to get a set of index cards to write down the scriptures that make an impact on your heart and that reveal aspects of your Father's character and grace and His promises to you. Pray for Holy Ghost revelation of how precious you are in God's eyes to burn in your spirit.

It is God's actions that always convince me of His thoughts and feelings about me, His Church, His body, His children, and of you.

God, our Heavenly Father, sacrificed His only son, Jesus, to come down to earth and die in our place (John 3:16). He gave us His Holy Spirit as our guide and puts at our disposal legions of angels to do our bidding.

It is important that you declare the very words that God speaks over you. God's angels, whom He has positioned to watch over your affairs, are anxiously waiting to carry out your commands and war on your behalf. Although the subject of angels at our disposal warrants its own teaching, God's angels are always ready to minister to us.

> *Are not the angels all ministering spirits (servants) sent out in the service [of God for the assistance] of those who are to inherit salvation?*
> *Hebrews 1:14 (AMP)*

What God did in John 3:16 tells me that His considerations of you and me are very high. Have you ever been in a relationship, whether friendship or intimate, in which the other person tells you that they love you and how much you mean to them, yet when you look at their actions, the things they say and do always end up hurting you? When there is free time or the holidays roll around, would they rather go somewhere else or do things that do not involve you? If their actions are contrary to what they are speaking, it leaves you no other choice but to think otherwise—they are selfish, they do not love you, they do not care. The result of their actions, undoubtedly, will leave you feeling insecure and unloved.

I'm reminded of the actions of a young man during a Dayton, Ohio shooting. As the video captures the crowd running from the gunshots, the young man's girlfriend tripped and fell. In an instant, without a moment's thought, he showed the ultimate display of love. He jumped on top of his girlfriend and used his body to shield her from the gunman who was just a few yards away. Imagine that!

What would you have done? Would you protect someone, knowing it means losing your life? Not many people will do that.

Jesus did!

Jesus went above and beyond that for you. He not only took the bullets for you, but He took your sins and all your suffering. He paid the price for you. He traded everything negative that was headed your way, stood in the gap and took it all so that you can live a long and abundant life just as God, your Father, intended from the beginning of time.

Your Heavenly Father's thoughts for you are in the area of blessing, healing, deliverance, and holiness. Yes, I will continue to make the statement throughout this book that God wants you blessed, healed, delivered, and living a victorious and holy life.

Imagine, all the pressures you feel right now, all the labels and ungodly concepts people want to place on you, all the fighting, the strife, the things that are weighing you down—Jesus took all that and so much more for you when He went to the cross. His regard for you was that great.

You need to know that God loves you so much and thinks so much of you that if you were the only person in the world in need of saving, He would have gone through it all, the exact same suffering on the cross, just for you alone. He lets us know this in the parable in Matthew 18:12-14 about the shepherd who left the 99 sheep to go out in search of the one lost sheep.

Know who you are in Christ. Know His intentions for you by reading His word. Study His word, believe it, and don't doubt. Meditate upon God's word and let it sink into your mind, spirit and soul until the Holy Spirit reveals and anchors it deep in your core that you are a child of God, blessed and highly favored, until you know nothing else but that one glorious fact.

That is exactly who you are—blessed and highly favored of God. You are His beloved.

God Has Regarded You

If you have not accepted Christ as your Savior or if you have strayed away, whatever the situation is, take this moment right now to let Him know that you are willing to receive the work that He did on the cross for you. Thank God for that. For the price that Jesus paid with His Blood to set you free from everything. Bring yourself under His Blood and into covenant with Christ. Once you do, you can immediately claim His benefits, your blessings and inheritance as God's child and a joint heir with Christ Jesus. You can immediately synchronize your thoughts with His, and line up with His plans for your life—your destiny.

If you fully obey the Lord your God and carefully follow all his commands I give you today, the Lord your God will set you high above all the nations on earth.
Deuteronomy 28:1

Personal/Additional Notes:
_____
_____
_____
_____
_____
_____
_____
_____

Personal/Additional Notes:

CHAPTER 11
Prayer of Repentance

My Heavenly Father, I come to you today to ask your forgiveness for how I have lived my life up to this point. Forgive me for not trusting in Your word. Forgive my aimless wanderings when Your truth has been right here all along.

I declare from this moment forward that I belong to You. I am Yours. I accept the work that Jesus did by His death on the cross as payment for my sins.

I confess my sins, the words I have spoken against You, and I receive and declare that I am now forgiven and covered by the Blood of Your Son, my Savior, Jesus Christ. From this moment forward, as Your child, I trust You and put my life and the lives of my loved ones into Your hands.

I choose to walk in the path that You have set before me. I choose life today. Life and blessings as You have instructed me in Deuteronomy 28.

I declare that all the attacks upon my life, my joy, my provisions and anything pertaining to the affairs of my life and the lives of my loved ones, end today. From now on, I walk in Your favor, in Your blessings, and in Your glory.

I declare Numbers 6:24 over my life. That You bless me, that Your light and Your favor are continually upon me and with that, I lack for nothing. I declare Psalm 91 over my life and that of my loved ones that from this day on we dwell under Your divine protection.

Heavenly Father, I declare that I am Your Beloved, and I choose to follow Your blueprint for my life as stated in Jeremiah 29:11 and Jeremiah 1:5.

I declare that as it is in Your Word, in Psalm 23:6, that is how it will always be for me and my family. So it shall be for my children and their children, for generations to come until the coming of our Lord and Savior, Jesus Christ.

Surely goodness and mercy shall follow us all the days of our lives from this day forward and forevermore (Psalm 23:6).

That is our expected end. Amen.

_____

Name

_____

Date

Prayer of Repentance

Feel free to write your own prayer of repentance and salvation now or you can come back to this page and do so later. Choose to trust God and abide by the agreement/prayer you set forth below. Make it your own and date it so that you always have a point of reference.

_____
_____
_____
_____
_____
_____
_____
_____
_____
_____
_____
_____
_____

_____
Name

_____
Date

Personal/Additional Notes:

CHAPTER 12
Renew Your Mind

17 Therefore if anyone is in Christ, he is a new creature; the old things passed away; behold, new things have come.
2 Corinthians 5:17

You have performed a reality check, identified who you really are and what you actually think of yourself. You have obtained a better perspective of where you are on the spectrum of your life compared to where God desires you to be. You have identified some blessing blockers and events in your life that led to and resulted in strongholds. You have come to the understanding that all these happenings and events that pull you contrary to God's word belong under the precious Blood of Jesus Christ. Most of all, you have looked at the truth of the matter, God's regard for you, which is the only view you need of yourself.

You now know, as I've stated over and over again in this book, that if you have identified a gap between where you are and where you need to be, start by aligning your thoughts and your words with that of your Heavenly Father. To do that, you need to renew your mind, change the way you think and adopt God's perspectives, which are clearly outlined in the Bible.

The Bible tells us in 2 Corinthians 5:17 that *if any man be in Christ, he is a new creature. Old things are passed away; all things have become new.* I urge you, therefore, to not continue to operate as that old self, who is already dead. Your new self now possesses the mind of Christ.

The Holy Spirit works in us to renew our minds through the Word of God. He teaches us. Our faith becomes strong, and we begin to act on it. It pours out of our hearts and changes our lives.

The root cause is in our old man, our old understanding, but we are renewed the moment we join ourselves with Christ.

Whatever the reason with the old self, be assured that there is now, nothing in your life that spending time with God and soaking in His presence will not resolve. Be assured that with Christ, you no longer need to condemn yourself of the past. Romans 8:1-2 *Therefore there is now no condemnation for those who are in Christ Jesus.* **2** *For the law of the Spirit of life in Christ Jesus has set you free from the law of sin and of death.*

There is nothing more beneficial than having quiet time with God. It needs to be a place where it is you and Him, no distractions, no televisions, radios, phones, social media—nothing—just you and God.

The enemy wants you to keep licking old wounds, keep you down and defeated and the recorder of your past playing over and over in your mind.

The Bible tells us in John 10:10 that the thief (Satan) comes to kill, steal and destroy; and that is exactly what he does. The enemy wants to kill God's children through calamity, steal their peace, joy, love, and tries to destroy them any way he can.

You need to press that supernatural stop button in your mind and get rid of evil words that others have spoken over you. Forget about things and actions that belonged to the old you.

Further on in John 10, we learn that the coming of Christ serves to give us fullness of life. When we come to God and give Him all that junk, He sets us free to believe, to love, to trust, and to be all that God expects us to be.

This is key to being whole again.

What it all boils down to is that you need to renew your mind in how you think, how you consider yourself, and then align your thinking with God's high regard for you.

Renewing your mind comes by spending time in His presence and in His word. When you sit in God's presence, it transforms you. Spending time with the Father enables you to solidify in your heart what God has already declared and decreed over you. Psalm 37:4 says, *Delight yourself in the Lord, and He will give you the desires of your heart.*

As you dwell in His presence, empty yourself of everything so that God is able to pour into your spirit the life He desires for you. In turn, when you ask a thing of God, you are asking Him for that which He has already downloaded into your spirit. Only through this can you begin to enjoy and experience a life above and beyond all that you could ask or imagine. Only by synchronizing your life with God can you walk in all His fullness.

Renewal of the mind is pivotal for a positional shift.

And do not be conformed to this world [any longer with its superficial values and customs], but be transformed and progressively changed [as you mature spiritually] by the renewing of your mind [focusing on godly values and ethical attitudes], so that you may prove [for yourselves] what the will of God is, that which is good and acceptable and perfect [in His plan and purpose for you].
Romans 12:2 (AMP)

Personal/Additional Notes:

_____
_____
_____
_____
_____
_____
_____
_____

CHAPTER 13
Know Who You Are In Christ

9 But you are a chosen race, a royal priesthood, a holy nation, a people for God's own possession, so that you may proclaim the excellencies of Him who has called you out of darkness into His marvelous light; 10 for you once were not a people, but now you are the people of God; you had not received mercy, but now you have received mercy.
1 Peter 2:8-10

Knowledge is power. Know who you are as a child of God. If you do not know who you are in God, how will you know His blessings apply to you? How can you walk in that which God has prepared for you?

You have now seen how God regards you and that He loves you and wants the best for you. He wants you to prosper in everything you do: in your job, at home, your business, your ministry, and wherever you go.

Knowledge is power! Knowledge of who you are in Christ is the tool to unlocking the door to the life God desires you to live.

Not only do you need to know it, you need to believe it in your heart.

Renewing your mind with the knowledge of who you are is the key to changing your thinking and opening the door to taking control of your life.

Don't go through life without grasping the truth and depth of who you are as a child of God and the power behind you. You would be like a king or president who does not grasp the extent of his authority and the forces and troops at his command.

When the revelation of your position in Christ drops into your spirit and gets grafted into your being, nothing will be unreachable. You will be unstoppable, and nothing will be impossible nor will anything be able to stand against you.

17 so that Christ may dwell in your hearts through faith; and that you, being rooted and grounded in love, 18 may be able to comprehend with all the saints what is the breadth and length and height and depth, 19 and to know the love of Christ which surpasses knowledge, that you may be filled up to all the fullness of God.
Ephesians 3:17-19

CHAPTER 14
Know the Power In His Blood

18 knowing that you were not redeemed with perishable things like silver or gold from your futile way of life inherited from your forefathers, 19 but with precious blood, as of a lamb unblemished and spotless, the blood of Christ. 20 For He was foreknown before the foundation of the world, but has appeared in these last times for the sake of you 21 who through Him are believers in God, who raised Him from the dead and gave Him glory, so that your faith and hope are in God.
1 Peter 1:18-20

Hell hath no fury that God has not extinguished on the cross through the death and Blood of Jesus Christ. The Blood of Jesus is the most powerful weapon of mass destruction in your arsenal.

All your hurts, rejections, destructive emotions and the losses and abuse belong under His Blood. The very Blood that Jesus shed when He was nailed to the cross at Calvary, crucified and died, all because of you and me.

There is nothing that is happening, has happened to you or that you have done that you cannot bring under the Blood of Jesus Christ. The Blood of our Lord and Savior, Jesus Christ, has cleansing and healing properties and the power to take you through whatever it is you are going through. The Blood heals, protects, strengthens, imparts knowledge, justifies and lays out all of God's provisions for His children. Every blessing you need, want or desire, is under His Blood.

We read in Leviticus 17:11 that it is the blood that makes atonement for one's life. Jesus' Blood not only cleanses us from our sins, it saves us from hell and damnation and brings us under His covering unto righteousness.

Jesus encourages you to come to Him as you are, hurt and broken. Not only does He invite you to come and tell Him about your problems, your hurts, your lack, but He longs for you to come and find rest in Him and receive His healing and peace.

One of the things I do, especially when I need healing (doesn't matter what kind of healing), is to anoint the water in my house, including my shower. I declare that the water that runs through my house represents the Blood of Christ and contains all the healing properties and power that is in His Blood. If Jesus can turn water into wine, why not my water into His precious Blood. I have the confidence that as I take a drink of water, shower, etc., it represents His Blood and I can receive healing.

Strange? I think not.

The man at Bethesda (John 5) and many others would wait by the pool until the angel of the Lord stirred up the water. The very first person who entered the pool would immediately be healed.

Peter's shadow and handkerchiefs were mediums that God used to provide healing. Yes, the supernatural realm is real, and it works.

There are naturopaths and holistic methods as well as pharmaceutical methods of healing. God is the healer, Who also provides wisdom, to mankind, for healing.

Jesus said that greater things than He has done will we do—He spat, made mud and healed the blind man. We bless and then drink juice/wine as a representation of His Blood and eat a wafer as the representation of his body.

Never underestimate the power that is in His Blood.

For He made Him who knew no sin to be sin for us, that we might become the righteousness of God in Him.
2 Corinthians 5:21

Personal/Additional Notes:

CHAPTER 15
Annihilate Your Gideon Complex

The angel of the Lord appeared to him and said to him, "The Lord is with you, O valiant warrior.
Judges 6:12

Gideon is one of my favorite characters in the Bible. Perhaps you might see yourself, or a part of you, in Gideon as we go through his story, which starts in chapter six of the book of Judges.

Gideon was a young man who lived after the time of the mighty miracles and wonders God performed when He delivered the Israelites and brought them out of Egypt.

When we first meet Gideon, he is not out in the open, doing business as usual. Instead, he is hiding in a cave as he performs simple, daily chores.

When God's angel appeared to Gideon, he greeted Gideon with one of the greatest compliments ever, even though the angel did not find Gideon standing brave, chest puffed out, cape draped over his shoulders and ready to defend his people.

As we see in Judges 6:12, when the angel of the Lord appeared to Gideon, he said, *"The Lord is with you, mighty warrior."*

What a compliment, and that from an angel, taking into consideration that angels know the full extent of what it takes to be a mighty warrior and fight battle after battle.

I imagine Gideon peered into that dark cave to see what young man of valor was hiding there, for surely the angel was not referring to him, Gideon, as a mighty warrior. A warrior is someone who is willing to protect, defend, and even fight to the death for his people and his country. Yet, this angel had walked into that cave and addressed Gideon as a mighty one at that.

So how does this mighty warrior respond? He asks, *"Pardon me, my lord, but if the Lord is with us, why has all this happened to us? Where are all His wonders that our ancestors told us about when they said, 'Did not the Lord bring us up out of Egypt?'"*

Gideon takes it one step further as he justifies why his people are in hiding, and like most Christians, he dares to play the "Blame it on God Game" for the situations in which they find themselves. Gideon accuses God by saying, *"But now the Lord has abandoned us and given us into the hand of Midian."*

Where did Gideon and his people get the notion that God had abandoned them? If God seems far away or absent, guess who moved or played the disappearing act?

Hint: Not God.

The angel was relentless and once again said to Gideon, *"Go in the strength you have."* Note the three things the angel mentioned Gideon was:

1. a mighty man of valor,
2. God was with him, and
3. he possessed strength.

Really? Gideon was all that? He possessed valor and strength and God was with him?

That mighty warrior did not think so, though. Like you and me, he wants to know the why, instead. If God is with me, then why, why, why? If God is so good, then where are the miracles, where are my blessings, my healings, the promotions, the more than enough, the above and beyond He promised?

Gideon was focused on his situation, his position, and the suffering of his people. Gideon "existed" in the problem, the circumstance and his status. Gideon was not expecting God to come and deliver them. No one else was, so why should he? I do not blame Gideon one bit. Although he was aware of the history of his people, if he grew up hearing that God had abandoned His own people, how was Gideon expected to rise above their current situation?

Gideon's environment was not conducive for bravery or prosperity of any kind.

Gideon was at a place where I have been before, and I'm positive you have as well.

He declared with confidence his thoughts about himself. He had already considered who he was and was certain of it; yet we see that Gideon's thoughts were contrary to the "mighty man of valor" he was in God's eyes.

Just like you and I do sometimes: Instead of aligning our thoughts with God's thoughts, we think we are not strong enough for the battle, we're not smart enough for the task or challenge ahead.

"Where is God?" we ask, forgetting He has provided all we need for the battle, and furthermore, has given us victory through His Son, Jesus and His death on the cross. We dare to ask where is God when we have failed to include and ask Him in the affairs of our lives.

Allow me to paraphrase and outline Gideon's justification of how he saw himself.

1. Gideon's people were no longer the great Israelites feared by many.
2. Among the 12 tribes that make up the Israelite nation, Gideon's tribe, the tribe of Manasseh, was at the bottom of the totem pole.
3. Of the tribe of Manasseh, his family, the Abiezrites, was the weakest, and
4. He, Gideon, a nobody.

In essence, what Gideon conveyed to the angel was that he was of little or no importance or power at all. He had no clout—he was nothing.

Wowsers! Talk about a quadruple, negative view of one's self. It is apparent that Gideon did not know who he was in God nor that he had God's power behind him, backing him up all the way.

Growing up as a young boy, I'm sure Gideon observed the severe persecutions of the Israelites. Despite the many stories he had heard of God's deliverance, and we know from Judges 6:13 that Gideon knew of those victorious moments in God. He was persuaded to believe the worst because, instead of standing up to their enemies and trusting in the God of their great generals, Abraham, Isaac, Jacob, Joseph, and Moses—instead of trusting in God's defense, Gideon and his people chose to cower and hide.

The Israelites were a nation who trusted God for deliverance from slavery and actually saw, with their own eyes, God split the Red Sea, and then close it again to swallow up their enemies.

So how did the Israelites come from such a victorious people who were revered and feared by those around them to a people afraid and hiding in caves?

Their story, the reason for their demise, which occurred after 40 years of peace after Deborah's victory of Canaan, was the consequence of their disobedience and evil ways. God called them out on this in Judges 6:10 and told them "...*you did not listen to Me.*"

So, what we see here, is proof that disobedience is a blessing blocker, a stronghold that can cause you to get stuck or digress from God's blueprint for your life.

Was there not one among the twelve tribes of Israel who could stand up for God and defend His Name and His people? We have seen over and over again in the Bible that all God needs is one individual daring enough to trust Him and bold enough to take on the challenge.

Do you feel God has abandoned you? Do you feel that God's divine protection is no longer upon your life? Sadly enough, that is the thought many Christians have today.

This is so true of many believers who have already considered themselves, as did Gideon, to be far less than the person whom God would answer or willingly bless, let alone the one God would choose to save their family, their neighborhood, their workplace, or their nation.

We have considered that we are striving to get somewhere in our walk with God, that we have to fight for every step we take; and to get there we need to hide in the shadows, in caves, dig holes and go underground like moles.

We have ascertained in our minds that there are positions in God that are reserved for great preachers and evangelists, but not for us. We think so because, like Gideon, we have considered that, of all Christians, my country, my state, my city, my county, my church is not known or on television and my family is the least in the church; and in my home, I am the black sheep.

We hide away in our little corners, trying to make it through life, telling God that when it's all over, we would be happy if we could just slide through the gates into heaven. We think we would be satisfied with just a little cottage when God, Himself, has for us a mansion and tells us so.

What Happens When You Know Who You Are?

I don't want to leave a bad impression of Gideon. Here's why I like him so much. Gideon allowed himself to be transformed into the vision God had of him. Let's see what happened once he got his stinking thinking straightened out.

That same night the LORD said to him, *"Take the second bull from your father's herd, the one seven years old. Tear down your father's altar to Baal and cut down the Asherah pole beside it. ^{26}Then build a proper kind of altar to the LORD your God on the top of this height. Using the wood of the Asherah pole that you cut down, offer the second bull as a burnt offering."* Judges 6:25

God was in essence instructing Gideon as to what he needed to do in order to save himself and his people. And those instructions are exactly what you need to do to save yourself and take control of your life once again.

When you fully realize who you are in Christ and the implication, the power, the impact it will make in changing things around for the better, you too, will quickly move to disconnect, disassociate, and denounce all dealings with the enemy. You will tear down all altars, strongholds, and anything that is not of God in your life.

Once you sever those ties to the enemy, repent and rededicate yourself to God. Give those areas of your heart and life that were once occupied with sin and evil to God. Superimpose the work on the cross/the blood of Jesus over things and people the enemy used to control your life.

In verse 27, we see that Gideon took ten of his servants and did as the LORD told him. But because he was afraid of his family and the townspeople, he did it at night rather than in the daytime.

It may seem scary and frightening to take that first step. If you need to, get connected with people who are on fire for God and ask their support.

I noticed that Gideon took ten of his servants and not friends. I'm speculating that the reason is because he can tell his servants what to do and they will do it, no questions asked. His friends, on the other hand, may have tried to talk him out of what he was about to do. I bring this up because when you need support on something God has instructed you to do, you don't ask people's opinions or permissions. You don't need naysayers. Get folks who will get on board and lend their support.

There are so many things I can touch on in just this one chapter. But here is my final point.

> *33 Now all the Midianites, Amalekites and other eastern peoples joined forces and crossed over the Jordan and camped in the Valley of Jezreel. 34 Then the Spirit of the LORD came on Gideon, and he blew a trumpet, summoning the Abiezrites to follow him. 35 He sent messengers throughout Manasseh, calling them to arms, and also into Asher, Zebulun, and Naphtali so that they too went up to meet them.*
>
> *Judges 6:33-35.*

You might ask why the Spirit of God fell on Gideon only now; why not earlier when he was in the winepress doing his chores?

What I see here, is that once Gideon destroyed the altar (door/channel of the enemy) and repented, the Spirit of the Lord was able to fall on Gideon and awaken the warrior within. Just look at him in chapters 34 & 35 as he tells the Abiezrite family to follow him, sending messages to Manasseh and calling others to prepare for battle.

Is this the Gideon whom we first met hiding in a cave?

Not only did Gideon's opinion of himself change, so did the people. They started calling him Jeru-Baal, which means idol-slayer. That is what happens when you let those things of the world go and allow God to take control. That is exactly what happens when the revelation of who you are as a child of God hits you. That warrior spirit is inside all of us. In case you don't sense it or know it, why don't you take account of the idols and altars in your life, tear them down and see what happens? I double-dare you!

Don't just think about it, write down your idols and altars, and then one by one, destroy them. Remove them from your life. Once you do, get ready for a fresh anointing, the unleashing of the warrior inside you.

It is no different today. It is the same thing that happened in Acts 1:8. You will receive the Power of God in your life when the Holy Spirit falls on you.

To wrap it up, get the revelation of your position in Christ. Know that there's a mighty warrior inside you waiting to be unleashed. God has already endowed and equipped you with strength to be victorious over every situation in your life.

Know that God is always with you. God's Spirit will come upon you to do mighty things, to be victorious, to be a conqueror and to live your most blessed life when you tear down the idols and Asherah poles in your life.

But you will receive power and ability when the Holy Spirit comes upon you; and you will be My witnesses [to tell people about Me] both in Jerusalem and in all Judea, and Samaria, and even to the ends of the earth.
Acts 1:8 (AMP)

Personal/Additional Notes:
_____
_____
_____
_____
_____
_____
_____
_____
_____
_____
_____
_____

CHAPTER 16
Spend Time In His Presence

2 Obey the king's command, I say, because you took an oath before God. 3 Do not be in a hurry to leave the king's presence.
Ecclesiastes 8:2-3 (NIV)

Be purposeful and determined to carve out time to get to know your Heavenly Father. How else are you expected to know Him if you do not spend time with God? Whether it is in reading and studying His word, praying or worshiping, develop a relationship with God. He is your Father. He loves you and cares for you.

It is in spending time with God, that He reveals His secrets to you, imparts wisdom and so much more. You get to learn about yourself, about the warrior within and talents you never knew you had when you wait in His presence.

Let me encourage you, once again, to have pen and paper ready when you meet with your Father. Gather information on what God says about you and how He regards you. Write down everything He tells you, those scriptures that are instrumental on how to live your life, and provide His promises. These are the foundational truths that will transform your life dramatically. My recommendation is that you turn that information into knowledge. Knowledge is knowing the fact (the truth) and value of the information presented.

Truth is a very valuable weapon and tool. It sets captives free. Jesus, knowing who He is, spoke that if He, as the son of God, sets us free, then we are free indeed (John 8:32). That freedom comes from spending time in Him and getting to know His word. In turn, you get to know who you truly are in Christ.

Time in God's presence leads to intimacy. David lived a life of intimacy with God. Psalm 119:164 tell us that David praised God seven times a day. To do that, David had to make a conscious effort to seek the face of God. That is desperation! That is desire! Why do I say desperation? That is because David was a man, a king in constant battle, but he also knew like some of us, if not most of us, that when we are in trouble, we call on God. Even unbelievers know this fact and put it into action.

When the planes crashed into the Twin Towers of the World Trade Center in Manhattan, on a Tuesday morning on September 11th, 2001, there was standing room only in almost every Church in the United States that next day. Churches which hardly filled their front pews for Wednesday night prayer, were suddenly packed to beyond capacity.

People tend to do that in the middle of a crisis; repent, turn back to God and cry out to Him for help.

Intimacy is you coming to God, seeking fellowship with Him even when things are going great in your life. It is developing a relationship with Him, in the good times and in the bad times; getting to know Who He really is and who you really are and what He is all about. It is not a one-time deal or a once-in-a-while love affair. It is a constant connection.

When you are intimate with someone, you get to find out a lot about them; more importantly, you get to know their heart's intentions for you.

In your case, God has provided you many ways to get to know Him and to find out His desires for you. It is all spelled out in the Bible.

Great men and women of God, such as Katherine Kuhlman, William J, Seymour, John G. Lake, Maria Woodworth Etter, and Evan Roberts, desired for God to totally consume them.

After serving God and doing mighty wonders in His name for years, and giving up a multi-million-dollar career in the 1800s to follow God, John G. Lake continuously cried out for more of God and to see more of God's power and glory. Oh, that you and I would cry out for more of God in our lives. What a transformation that would be!

Being totally surrendered to and intimate with God means having to wake up early or going to bed late, turning off the television, the cell phone and all of today's gadgets and gizmos, and technology, to spend time with God. When you do, you will get to know the heart of God and His expectations for you.

Here is a challenge for you. Invite God into your day-to-day activities. Dare to carve out time like David did and see how many times a day you praise God.

Decide whether to allocate times in your day or alternate your days to do the following activities:

- read the Bible, study what God says so you know the truth for yourself. As you study the Bible,
- write down (on index cards) your inheritance/legacy and God's promises that belong to you,
- pray for your family's needs, the needs of others and the world,
- pray the promises you are now discovering,
- worship and praise God, and most importantly,
- meditate upon the scriptures and weave them into who you are; make them a part of your daily life.

It is in spending time in His presence, doing activities such as mentioned above that you can solidify who you really are in God and the power that you have backing you as His child.

> *But when you pray, go into your most private room, close the door and pray to your Father who is in secret, and your Father who sees [what is done] in secret will reward you.*
> *Matthew 6:6*

CHAPTER 17
Meditate On And Speak His Word

*This Book of the Law shall not depart from your mouth, but you shall read [and meditate on] it day and night, so that you may be careful to do [everything] in accordance with all that is written in it; for then you will make your way prosperous,
and then you will be successful.*
Joshua 1:8 (AMP)

We are forced to come to our own conclusions about things, situations, and ourselves when we do not meditate upon God's word and seek His counsel. God instructed the Israelites to meditate on His word and hang it on their doorposts as a reminder.

6 These words, which I am commanding you today, shall be on your heart. 7 You shall teach them diligently to your sons and shall talk of them when you sit in your house and when you walk by the way and when you lie down and when you rise up. 8 You shall bind them as a sign on your hand and they shall be as frontals on your forehead. 9 You shall write them on the doorposts of your house and on your gates (Deuteronomy 6:6-9).

Bring yourself into alignment with the Word of God. Do not let anyone write the script for your life. God has already designed the blueprint for you to follow. It is in His word.

As you do the above challenge and spend time and study the Bible, you will discover God's intentions. These promises are what you need to meditate on, speak out, and align to your life. In doing so, you will protect His anointing upon your life. Do not allow man-made words, rules and regulations, and religion to destroy the foundation God is building. Take those things you have gathered from your intimate time with God and read and meditate upon them. God's Holy Spirit will make it real to you. These are the truths of God's words and what you need to set you free.

Fill your heart with the expectation of God's promises and let it spill out of your mouth and over into your life. Speaking what God has already declared of you is vital to living a life of abundance.

Your heavenly Father has angels at your disposal, eagerly waiting for you to speak His words, giving them (God's angels) the command to go and get you what it is you need. Too many of us, leave our angels idle when they could be working on our behalf to get things done.

Meditate On And Speak His Word

Bless (affectionately, gratefully praise) the Lord,
you His angels, you mighty ones who do His
commandments, hearkening to the voice of his word.
Psalm 103:20 (AMP)

Once again, do not let the stinking thinking of others be the coordinates in your GPS. Let God's word be the trajectory to your destiny.

Words are weapons of massive destruction; whether they are used to build up or tear down and destroy, they are very powerful. Our spoken words are so powerful that they can make or break us. (Ephesians 4:29-32). The words you speak can open the doors for outpoured blessings in your life or shut them closed for good. Are the words you are currently speaking, bringing death to your finances, job, business, marriage, family? Use your God-given GPS, your tongue, to get you to arrive exactly at your destination, next level up, wherever your heart desires to go, and more importantly, where God wants you to be.

God used words to create the universe. He spoke things into existence, and the world formed. You may say, but that is God. He is the Creator. True, but are we not made in His image? Did not Jesus commission us to do greater things than He did? So, if Jesus healed the blind, deaf and dumb with His words and cursed a fig tree causing it to wither and die with His words, are we not to use our words to benefit and bless ourselves, our families, our environment, our nation?

I recommend that you pin the scriptures and thoughts from your prayer time on your mirror, dashboard, computer, refrigerator, to daily remind you of who you are in Christ. Surround yourself with the word for the simple fact that many times after our personal time with God, like the man in the mirror, we step away and forget who we are. So, I encourage you to put up little reminders at places that you frequent during the day.

One of my favorite scriptures is taped to my computer monitor. It is Psalm 119:147 – *I rise early to cry out for help and to put my hope in Your words.* It encourages me every day when I sit down to start my day's work that I am totally dependent on Him for my day's blessings and direction.

The one thing that remains constant no matter who you are, what you're going through, your background, status, and the labels the world chooses to identify you, is that God has already declared you blessed and highly favored.

How blessed is the man
who does not walk in the counsel of the wicked,
Nor stand in the path of sinners, Nor sit in the seat
of scoffers! 2 But his delight is in the law of the
Lord, And in His law he meditates day and night.
3 He will be like a tree firmly planted by streams of
water, Which yields its fruit in its season And its leaf
does not wither; And in whatever he does, he prospers.
Psalm 1:1-3

CHAPTER 18
See It How God Sees It

Blessed be the God and Father of our Lord Jesus Christ, who hath blessed us with all spiritual blessings in heavenly places in Christ: 4 According as he hath chosen us in him before the foundation of the world, that we should be holy and without blame before him in love: 5 Having predestinated us unto the adoption of children by Jesus Christ to himself, according to the good pleasure of his will, 6 To the praise of the glory of his grace, wherein he hath made us accepted in the beloved.
Ephesians 1:3-6

So far, you've assessed your current situation, looked at triggers that may have opened doors to the enemy, hopefully identified blessing blockers that are holding you up from receiving and walking in the fullness of God. Greater yet, you have discovered God's thoughts and how He regards you.

This is the way I see it. Before you accepted Christ as your Savior, you were eternally separated from God and all His blessings for you. Even if you were living a life of comfort and riches, you were still eternally separated from God's choicest blessings for your life. Yet the minute you realized that you were a sinner, lost without God, damned to hell for eternity, and needing a Savior, the moment you asked for forgiveness of your sins and welcomed Christ into your life as your Lord and King, something beyond spectacular happened.

That chasm between you and God was instantly removed, gone forever. In one split second, Jesus took a big step and embraced you, engulfed you in everything that He is. You were instantly stripped of everything that you were and immediately adorned in His likeness in every way (Ephesians 1:3).

Imagine this, your spirit is changed, enveloped in everything Christ is, and yet, it doesn't stop there. When Jesus embraces you, you become intertwined so tightly with Him that no one can distinguish you apart from Him.

Then, He, Jesus, goes and does something even more spectacular: He lifts you up high into the heavens and sits you down in heavenly places in Himself, Christ Jesus (Ephesians 2:6).

Everything Christ is, you now are in Him.

Do you get the picture? Neither your situation, nor your status, nor your race or ethnic background dictates who you are. You are exactly who Christ says you are. We have already explored this in previous chapters.

Gideon had already considered himself a loser because his people struggled under the hands of the Midianites and Amalekites. They were being greatly oppressed; their dignity, respect, and sustenance constantly being taken from them. They survived by hiding in caves. That is no way to live. It is mere existence. They were existing like total losers. No wonder Gideon didn't think much of himself—but again, who would?

Notice, however, God did not come to Gideon and ask him to start training and building himself up. God did not send angels to give Gideon pep talks. Gideon did not attend motivational seminars. God had already considered Gideon a mighty warrior; therefore, there was no need for God to require Gideon to do any preparations to get himself ready for the battles ahead.

God asked Gideon to go in the strength that he, Gideon, already possessed—to go in the strength of who Gideon was in God. Gideon did not know his position or the power behind him, but all of heaven knew.

Here is one great fact to convince you of how highly God thinks of you. The fact that God gave up his only Son, Jesus Christ, to be ridiculed, humiliated, stripped of all His glory, and crucified just to save you tells me that God had high considerations of you.

How about that? If I asked you now, at this point in the book, to write a few sentences about yourself and how you measure up in accordance with God's Word for your life, what would you write?

_____
_____
_____
_____
_____
_____

    Whether you can see the manifestation now or not does not matter. You do not have to see it to believe it. The belief must start in your head and flow into your heart; believe it first and then you will see it manifest and come to light in your daily walk.

    You should by now realize just how precious you are, and that God considers you of great worth. Society has not made a place for you in this world, God has. Perhaps now, despite all the turmoil(s) you have gone through, the tragedies and mishaps in your life, you are beginning to think differently. Instead of asking why, you now realize like Gideon, that you are a mighty warrior and that God is with you.

    When my husband and I got married, the Church we attended was just as wonderful and loving as my church in New York, but the belief system was a little different—well, way different to be honest. It was prayer meeting night, and I was looking for a job, and my request was for God to provide gainful employment where I could earn double the minimum wage per hour. All I was looking for was

$8/$10 per hour rather than the $5/$6 being offered at the unemployment agency.

Now, at the time, we were living in a little resort/college town. After prayers, the pastor had a word with me and explained that my expectations were too high. He proceeded to share how he had humbled himself while going to seminary school, earning minimum wage to support his family.

Well, I listened to him, but my mind was already made up. I had always believed God wanted to give me His best and whatever my heart desired. In fact, my motto at the time was that as soon as I begin to think and meditate upon a thing, God provides it.

Needless to say, I went to my job interview and proposed my expectations for the company. Instead of being offered what I had prayed for, God did over and above my request. The company told me they couldn't hire me. Instead, if I would bring my skills to them and generate the business that would open the position I was seeking, they would split their profits with me 50/50.

You can imagine my shock. I started out of the gate making ten times above and beyond my expectations. And of course, I had to go back and give my report that God provided over and above my expectations. I shared this not to boast, but to prove that God wants His children blessed.

There is nothing wrong in making a big deal of Who your Father is and wanting God's best for your life. Do not let others direct you away from the path God has for you or from thinking God wants the best for you.

Some still did not get it and attributed it to mere luck. Luck is for doubters and unbelievers. Faith and the benefits of believing are for God's children—believers. Luck is something you have to strive for, a hit or miss thing. Unlike luck, the blessings of God are permanent and always available, an inheritance received that can never be annulled.

People are not always going to get it, but you need to move on in God, never doubting, but always believing that you have received that which God has outlined for you in His word.

I do not bother disputing the issue with those who do not believe in the promises of God. They have come too late to convince me otherwise. Trying to prove to them that the blessings of God are for His beloved would be like casting my precious pearls to pigs.

I have already tried God and proved Him to be true to every word He spoke. He wants me blessed. He wants His children blessed. He wants you blessed.

So, whether you are being moved to change your beliefs or you do not think God's blessings apply to you, study the scriptures to show yourself approved of what God can do (2 Timothy 2:15).

I cannot stress it enough. Study and meditate on God's word and you will receive instant revelation though His

Holy Spirit, and receive instant change in your belief system.

Many studies have shown that for adults to believe and learn a new thing, they have to see it, hear it, speak it, and then write it. Studies also show that it takes 30 days of being consistent to change a habit or implement a new habit or belief system (2 Corinthians 5:17). But again, that is man's ways.

I find that very funny because long before the scientists spent millions of dollars on this research, God documented all these principles in His best seller, *the Bible*.

So, it does not matter what you think or what position you're in now. The way I see it, if you desire change, transformation, a better life—whatever that means to you, there is hope. It is not too late to change, renew your mind and live your best life.

He made Him who knew no sin to be sin on our behalf, so that we might become the righteousness of God in Him.
2 Corinthians 5:12

Personal/Additional Notes:

CHAPTER 19
Shift Your Paradigm

2 And do not be conformed to this world [any longer with its superficial values and customs], but be transformed and progressively changed [as you mature spiritually] by the renewing of your mind [focusing on godly values and ethical attitudes], so that you may prove [for yourselves] what the will of God is, that which is good and acceptable and perfect [in His plan and purpose for you].
Romans 12:2

Merriam-Webster defines a paradigm shift as an important change that happens when the usual way of thinking about or doing something is replaced by a new and different way.

This is the same meaning and concept the Bible talks about in Romans 12:2 as we are encouraged to renew (shift/change) our minds from worldly views and assumptions and adopt the principles and theories of God.

All is not lost. God provides a comeback for us, and boy, do I love comebacks. I think everyone does. Imagine the hero/heroine in a movie, the underdog, the trodden and beaten down who is missing out or doesn't get how to survive or rise above their circumstances. We root for them because we want them to win; and when they finally get it and we see them succeed, we are elated.

Samson lost through disobedience, but he made a big comeback in the end; and we see, that on his last day, he defeated and killed more Philistines than ever before. Samson knew that despite his mess-up, the power of God was still in operation in his life. He knew that if He called on God, He would answer, and that is exactly what God did—Samson called, God responded.

Some individuals in the Bible would never have nominated themselves as apt to take on a quest for God. Yet, as you read their stories, you cannot help but see how, by taking on a new mindset, they went on to be great champions for God.

Regardless of who in the Bible you identify with, you, too, can make a comeback.

Now unto Him that is able to do exceeding abundantly above all that we can ask or think, according to the power that worketh in us.
Ephesians 3:20

It is worth repeating that you need to step into and walk in all that God has already reserved for you. In order to renew your mind, you need to set aside time to spend with God, reading His Word, meditating and feasting on His promises so that you can walk in His provisions and blessings. I urge you not to miss out on what God has stored up for you and your family. It would be sad to get to the end of your life and realize that all you lost was simply because of lack of knowledge. It is a no-brainer if all you have to do is repeat what He, God, has already spoken over you.

You can meditate upon the scriptures as you are driving around town, going to work, wherever you are, in the shower, as you are lying down waiting for sleep to come. Meditation translates the Word of God (the logos word) to God's direct words (made alive) to you (the rhema word). When you reflect on the scriptures, it becomes part and parcel of your nature and thereby changes the way you think. Meditating on the Word of God enables you to develop and have the mind of Christ. The Holy Spirit in us teaches and reveals this to us.

Another one of my favorite verse is in Ecclesiastes 8:3. We are urged to be patient and not be in a rush to leave the presence of the King. You are going to get rid of a lot of junk at His feet, when you stay and linger in His presence.

You don't need to hide in caves like Gideon did nor do you need to be afraid of what's happening in the world. God has already provided His covering for you, under His shadow as mentioned in Psalm 91. That is His promise to you, His child—you have the entire host of heaven as your army, your secret service men and at your command. They go before you into a job, a shopping mall, and everywhere.

I am a big believer in using the power of the tongue, to speak God's word to bring about change. If you begin to do that, you will see the blessing of God manifest all around you every day.

Who satisfies your desires with good things so that your youth is renewed like the eagle's.
Psalm 103:5

Personal/Additional Notes:
_____
_____
_____
_____
_____
_____
_____
_____
_____
_____
_____
_____
_____

CHAPTER 20
Expect "An Expected End"

For I know the thoughts that I think toward you, saith the Lord, thoughts of peace, and not of evil, to give you an expected end.
Jeremiah 29:11

Expect the life you live from this moment on (until Jesus calls you home) to be filled with His blessings, provisions, and promises. Dare to believe and collect on God's promises. Surely, His goodness and mercy will follow and pursue you to the end of your days. That is God's promise to you and to me. Expect it and live it.

I hope I have provided you with sufficient evidence to show you how important it is to line up your thinking and your speech with the way God thinks and speaks about you. God regards you highly.

I am so glad that God arrested me and, through His Holy Spirit, taught me the power in changing my thoughts and my words and aligning them to His word, reflecting His regard for me in the words that I speak over my life. It totally turned my life 180 degrees.

There are so many scriptures that tell us how God expects us to end. First, our end in this life is only the beginning of eternal life; but while you're waiting to enter into that eternal realm, He promises to satisfy you with good things so that your youth is renewed like that of an eagle's (Psalm 103:5).

If you take nothing from this book, take away the knowledge that God has stated in his Word, the Bible, that He wants you blessed. Believe and implement that in your life. It will catapult you to new heights, new levels, and new dimensions.

I encourage you to allow the concepts in this book to sink into your spirit. I challenge you to set aside the next 30 days and put into practice the principles you have learned here. Know and believe God loves you. Spend time and get to know Him and His word. Meditate on and speak what God has declared over you.

You are blessed and highly favored of God.

The Lord bless you, and keep you; The Lord make His face shine on you, And be gracious to you; The Lord lift up His countenance on you, And give you peace.
Numbers 6:24

www.ingramcontent.com/pod-product-compliance
Lightning Source LLC
Chambersburg PA
CBHW030153100526
44592CB00009B/263